THE
RETIREMENT
SUCCESS

Solution

&

Lessons I Learned from the Past Bear Market

*A*dvantage™
PERSONAL FINANCE

E. RONALD LARA, CFP

The Retirement Success Solution & Lessons I Learned from the Past Bear Market by E. Ronald Lara, CFP®
Copyright © 2011 by E. Ronald Lara
All rights reserved.
ISBN: 978-1-59755-100-7

Published by: ADVANTAGE BOOKS™
                www.advbookstore.com

Library of Congress Control Number: 2011937613

First Printing: October 2011
11 12 13 14 15 16 17 9 8 7 6 5 4 3 2 1
Printed in the United States of America

Acknowledgements

I wish to thank my contributing authors T.J. Doremus for his chapter on Retirement Planning for Special Needs Families; WendyAnn Payne for her chapter on Women and Retirement Planning; and Sterling Neblett CFP® for his work on The Retirement Success Solution® chapter.

I would especially like to thank Don Johnson, founder of The Business Word, for taking time to read the first draft and making recommendations which have been incorporated into this book. In addition, I'm grateful to Jennifer Szaro and Allison Baum for their help in editing this book as well as my wife, Patrice, for all of her help and encouragement in writing and editing this book.

Lastly, I would like to thank my clients who have placed so much trust in me and my firm over the past 40 years of my wonderful career as a financial planner.

Table of Contents

What to Look For in a Financial Advisor

Investment Product Overview

Conclusion: Making It All Work for You

E. Ronald Lara, CFP® - "The Retirement Coach"

This communication book is for information purposes only and should not be regarded as an offer to sell or as a solicitation of an offer to buy any security, investment product or service. Any information provided has been prepared from sources believed to be reliable but is not guaranteed and does not represent all available data necessary for making investment decisions. The contents herein reflect the opinion of the author and not that of Lara, Shull & May, LLC ("LSM"). Neither the author nor LSM shall be responsible for any trading decisions, damages or other losses resulting from or related to, this information data, analyses or opinions or their use. The advice and strategies contained herein may not be suitable for your situation. You should consult with a professional where appropriate.

Authors Bios

E. Ronald Lara, CFP®

With more than 40 years of financial planning experience, Ron has reached a point in his successful career where he now works primarily with high net-worth clients. He has become an expert on helping clients plan for their retirement goals and needs, all while using a philosophy that revolves around staying active. Instead of retiring "cold turkey," spend time doing what you enjoy and delegate (or eliminate) everything else. His philosophy of determining the growth rate needed to achieve your retirement goals, as well as your lifetime goals, has enabled his clients to retire using a more conservative approach to investing than was previously thought possible.

A native of the Washington, D.C. area, Ron's interests and goals led him to the University of Maryland, where he graduated in 1968 with a Bachelor of Science in Civil Engineering. Ron worked for Humble Oil and Refining Company (Exxon Mobil) for a year before serving in the United States Army through April 1971.

Following his military service, Ron entered the financial services industry and in 1977 became one of the first designated Certified Financial Planners (CFP®) in the Washington, D.C. area. He then started his own firm in 1981 which later became Lara, Shull & May, LLC ("LSM").

During the mid-80's, in an on-going attempt to maximize the investing power of his clients, Ron developed a strategy for purchasing U.S. Treasury Bonds, which prompted him in 1987 to formally start his Treasury Bond Management program. Following the success of this program, The Lara Group, Ltd. was formed in 1991 for the sole purpose of managing U.S. Treasury Bonds.

Today, Ron continues to serve as C.E.O. of Lara, Shull & May LLC, based in Falls Church, Virginia with offices in Frisco, Colorado and

Austin, Texas. LSM is a financial services planning firm that provides clients with a full range of investment, financial planning and specialized estate planning services. The firm has also developed, and offers, a set of helpful, proprietary online tools for investors. This includes the Lifetime Success Solution®, which is a comprehensive financial planning process that helps clients plan for and target for their financial and lifetime goals.

On a more personal side, Ron's many charitable affiliations have included memberships on the board of directors for The Fairfax Library Foundation, The Claude Moore Colonial Farm at Turkey Run, and Joe Gibb's Youth for Tomorrow. A devoted family man, Ron is married with five children and six grandchildren. His hobbies include skiing, flying, tennis and improving his golf game.

T.J. Doremus

A 1996 graduate of Hampden-Sydney College, T.J. has worked in the financial services industry for the past 10 years. He joined Lara, Shull & May, LLC in September of 2000. In his first year with the firm, T.J. was recognized as Elite Advisor by Alliance Capital and subsequently in 2001, 2002 and 2003. In 2003, T.J. was also named to the All-American Team by American Funds in recognition of his financial expertise and dedication to the principles of sound investing. In 2008, T.J. was recognized in New York by Reuters as TOP ADVISER 2008.

In June 2005, T.J. was selected as Washington D.C. area's first Protected Tomorrows™ Advocate and joined the Protected Tomorrows™ international network of elite independent advisors helping families plan for the future of their special needs children. In his work with special needs families, T.J. has been an exhibitor at the McLean Bible Church Accessibility Summit. He has worked in the special needs arena volunteering for different organizations for the past 15 years.

In addition, T.J. is the defensive coordinator for Langley High School's boys lacrosse team which has won back to back to back Virginia state high school lacrosse championships.

Sterling D. Neblett, CFP®

A 2005 graduate of James Madison University with a Bachelor of Business Administration in Finance and International Business, Sterling joined Lara, Shull & May, LLC in January 2007. Prior to joining LSM, Sterling worked as a Financial Advisor with NYLIFE Securities, Inc. where he achieved Executive Council in his first year of employment. In 2007, Sterling earned an Executive Certificate in Financial Planning after completing a rigorous 9-month continuing education study at Georgetown University. He is a Certified Financial Planner®.

Sterling is a member of LSM's Investment Committee and is responsible for investment analysis and selection for his team. In addition to working with Ron Lara's team, Sterling manages his own growing client base, specializing in retirement and estate planning as well as investments and insurance.

Wendy Ann Payne

Wendy joined Lara, Shull & May, LLC in January 2007. With over 11 years of experience in the securities industry, clients appreciate Wendy's being attuned to their individual needs as well as providing continuous stellar service. In addition to working with Ron Lara's team, Wendy manages her own growing practice, specializing in financial planning for women with an emphasis on financial education and awareness. She focuses on widows, divorcees, and other women who find themselves responsible for financial decisions for the first time in their lives. Wendy is a Certified Senior Advisor® (CSA).

Wendy resides in Lovettsville, Virginia with her husband, children and three dogs. She is actively involved within her community and also volunteers as an instructor for investment-related courses for the Fairfax County Adult Community and Education. She enjoys spending time with her family, scrapbooking, card-making, dancing, music, writing, traveling, and improving her gardening skills.

INTRODUCTION

There's no way around it: planning for retirement is a vitally important step in our lives. Our ability to continue to enjoy living, following a life's worth of work, depends upon it.

However, preparing for retirement can be marred by all kinds of obstacles and pitfalls, many of which are related to the actual process of saving the money needed to retire comfortably. Does it always have to be this way? Absolutely not, because there are things you can do (and need to do now) to make sure you have, at your disposal, the financial resources necessary when they are needed most.

For 40 years I have been working with clients helping them develop and implement effective tax, savings and investment strategies. Early in my career, my only concern was offering people investment plans designed to outpace inflation and provide some long-term growth. In the early '70s no one had heard of asset allocation. In short, the main idea was dollar cost averaging, which is the systematic investment of a specific dollar amount each month. For those individuals who invested in this manner, it lowered their average cost and rewarded them with impressive double-digit returns over the next 30 years.

As I worked more with older clients, people who were nearing or already at retirement age, I began to see they needed to move their investment efforts beyond the dollar cost averaging approach that was so popular during the '70s and '80s.

Throughout my career, financial-related forces – such as inflation, rising and falling interest rates, and rising/declining stock markets - have consistently been making a positive return on investments a difficult proposition. For example, during the early '80s high interest rates brought heavenly returns if you invested in fixed income investments such as government bonds, municipal bonds and mortgage-backed bonds. Case in point, during the early '80s government-backed Ginnie

Mae (Government National Mortgage Association)[1] bond yields peaked at 17% and money market funds yielded in excess of 20%, which is quite a contrast to the barely 0.10% yield on money market funds in 2010 (please see the Disclosure in the back of the book). Keep in mind, however, the high inflation rates that came along with this period acted as a negative long-term counterbalance to the money people thought they were making in these safe investment vehicles. In short, inflation was wiping out the purchasing power of the dollar.

From the mid-'80s through the 1990's, dramatically declining interest rates helped create one of the greatest Bull Markets in U.S. market history. Fueled by tech stocks and Y2K concerns, the Dow Jones Industrial Average, the S&P and the NASDAQ all posted unbelievable annual gains, all of which allowed investors to become accustomed to doubling and tripling their money within one to two years on tech stocks and/or "hot" internet start-ups.

By the mid-90's, I was approaching 25 years in the financial services field and started to see the value of determining the growth rates my clients needed to earn in order to achieve their lifetime goals, which typically amounted to anywhere from 5% to 8% on their investable assets. To make this happen, I counseled clients to look at, and utilize, more conservative investment vehicles and to use asset allocation to reach the growth rate needed to achieve their retirement goals.

Greed, however, was running rampant by the late-'90's and many clients were unhappy with even a 15% to 20% return, especially when their friends were doubling and tripling their money on high-flying equity holdings. Unfortunately, in March of 2000 the bubble burst and the biggest Bear Market since the Great Depression reared its ugly head. For example, the NASDAQ peaked at the 5,000 level in 2000, but in less than two years it declined 75%, the largest drop of any equity index in the history of the U.S. stock market.

Investors lost millions of dollars during this downturn by chasing astronomical returns in equities. I realized how important our strategy of determining the growth rate each individual needs to earn in order to achieve their lifetime goals had become. Even today, with market uncertainties brought about by a host of economic and political factors, my approach to investing has remained the same:

1. Help individuals and couples determine the spendable income they need to achieve a successful retirement.
2. Determine the gross income they will need by doing a thorough IRA distribution and tax analysis to determine from where to withdraw the income they need with the least amount of tax.
3. Complete our Retirement Funding Analysis to determine the growth rate needed to achieve that gross income goal.
4. Determine the asset allocation needed to achieve that goal with the least amount of risk.

(You can visit www.retirementsuccesssolution.com for more details.)

Why is it so important to determine the growth rate needed to achieve your retirement goals? The simple answer is this: **most investors take too much risk.** If a couple can achieve ALL of their lifetime and retirement goals by earning just 4%, WHY take the risk of investing in the equity markets? Instead, why not just invest in U.S. Treasury Bonds and government-backed mortgage bonds at 4.8% and 5.5% respectively (at the time of this writing)?

Never before was this approach more relevant than in the fall of 2008 when the U.S. and worldwide markets plummeted due to the collapse of the real estate markets. During this time, major brokerage firms, such as Bear Stearns and Lehmann Brothers, went under. Meanwhile, Merrill Lynch, the largest brokerage firm in the world, was forced to find a buyer over a weekend and Bank of America came to the rescue. Quasi-governmental firms such as Fannie Mae (Federal National Mortgage Association) and Freddie Mac (Federal Home Loan Association) collapsed, and major banks, such as Washington Mutual and Indy Bank, failed. General Motors had to file Chapter 11 bankruptcy. The Dow Jones Industrial Average dropped over 50% and people's retirement savings, which they had worked so hard to accumulate, were practically wiped out. However, for those who had invested in Ginnie Mae[1] and U.S. Treasury Bonds, their savings were secure.

This financial meltdown was brought on by the collapse of a speculative real estate market in which individuals could buy homes with no money down and finance 100% of the purchase cost. We did not learn the lessons of 1929 when the purchase of stocks on 5% margin ultimately led to the collapse of the stock market between 1929 and 1932 – the Dow Jones Industrial Average declined over 90%.

I have learned many lessons during the past 18 months, even though I had been through everything in my 40 years as a financial planner. In this book, I will share some of the lessons learned, in the hope that you will take them to heart and prosper.

It's hard to manage greed. While most of our clients have done very well, we have had our share of losses. While we participated in many successful real estate investments prior to 2005, two investments that we made in 2005 and 2006 were foreclosed in late 2007 and those investors lost that money. We are now utilizing tax and investment strategies to recover those losses in a tax efficient manner.

My point here is that very few financial advisors are right all of the time. However, if you follow the advice in this book you will have a much greater chance of having a successful retirement.

I will detail lessons learned in the past year – what worked, what didn't, and what you should look out for in the years to come.

In the real world, most people cannot expect to achieve their retirement goals with a growth rate of less than 5%. Given this, I encourage investors and other financial advisors to follow the strategies I have developed and used with great success. Bottom line, it is all about identifying a set of lifetime goals and then determining a growth rate needed on your investments to meet them. Is this possible in today's up-and-down marketplace? Yes, it is and I believe it can be accomplished by following a careful strategy that does two things: 1) determines the growth rate needed to achieve your retirement and lifetime goals; and 2) utilizes asset allocation targeted for your desired growth rate.

Great things are possible when it comes to saving for retirement. However, it takes careful planning and commitment to a solid strategy that remains focused on your lifetime goals. Are you up to the challenge? Are you ready to re-think your approach to retirement? These questions and more will need to be answered by the time you have completed this book.

Before you start to read this book, I encourage you to complete The Retirement Success Solution®2 scorecard at the end of the introduction (please see the Disclosure in the back of the book). It will give you a good idea of where you are and how much help you will need to achieve your lifetime goals.

As you go through the following chapters, I encourage you not only to read, but to get involved with the information I am sharing with you. Grab a pencil and paper and be ready to work, putting some careful thought into what the future holds. Simply reading the book but not doing the exercises or applying the information to your own situation will do you no good.

If after completing the scorecard and reading this book you feel overwhelmed, call your financial planner and ask for a detailed retirement plan that incorporates both the investment planning and the tax planning to achieve your retirement goals. If your current financial planner doesn't have the ability to do this consider finding a new financial planner that does. You can get a list of Certified Financial Planners (CFP®) in your area by going to http://www.cfp.net/search.

You can also call your accountant and ask them for a Certified Financial Planner® in your area whom they have worked with and have mutually satisfied clients.

With all this in mind, I wish you the best because your Retirement Success Solution®2 is right in front of you!

Retirement Success Solution® Scorecard

	1	2	3	4	5	6	7	8	9	10	
We don't have a clear vision of what we want to do in retirement.											We have a clear vision of what we want to do in retirement.
We don't have any idea of how much we will need in retirement.											We know how much income we will need in retirement.
We don't know where our income will come from.											We have complete knowledge of all income sources.
We don't know all the tax strategies available to us.											We are using tax strategies effectively to maximize our retirement
Our investments are scattered and disorganized.											Our investment portfolio is integrated and organized.
We don't know all the investment options and planning strategies available to us.											We have implemented the best investment strategies to reach our goals.
We don't review our vision, plan or progress on a regular basis.											We review our vision, plan or progress on a regular basis.
Our financial advisors work in isolation from each other.											Our financial advisors work as a team to help us achieve our vision.
We don't have the proper tax and financial plans in place to pass on our wealth.											We have the proper tax and financial plans in place to pass on our wealth.
We don't have as much confidence in the future as we would like.											We have a strong sense of confidence about the future.

Total Your Score:_____

85 – 100 Congratulations on your successful retirement!

65 – 84 You need to fine tune the planning you have done. A successful retirement can be yours with some additional tax and investment planning.

50 – 64 In order to have a successful retirement, you will need to do a fair amount of tax and investment planning.

Below 50 You may need an in-depth analysis to have a successful and enjoyable retirement.

CHAPTER ONE

Your Reasons for Retiring

Retirement is an admirable goal for everyone, no matter what your present (or expected) financial situation is. The key, though, is to first determine WHY you want to retire, not HOW you are going to retire.

So why do you want to retire, either now or later? Do you have a plan for what you are going to do when you retire? If so, does this plan take into account not only your financial needs, but your physical and mental ones as well? You have probably thought about the "upsides," but have you considered the "downsides" of retirement? These questions and more need to be considered and answered before you retire. Why? Well, your well being may depend upon it.

When working with clients, one of my first – and key – questions is, "Do you want to retire?" A common response is something like: "Well, I'm 65, so I guess I better." In my mind, there is no right or wrong answer because how you approach the issue of retirement depends on many different variables.

Unfortunately, I've known individuals who decided to retire at age 65 because they felt it was time or they worked for companies that had a mandatory retirement age. Too often, these people end up sitting around watching television all day, and not surprisingly they aren't happy about retirement. They gain weight and become sedentary, and some pass away in their early seventies, despite a history of long life in their family.

I have a client (who we will call Joe) who used to work for a real estate company. He has invested with me over the past 20 years, reaping the benefits of the rising stock market of the 1980's and 1990's. By the summer of 2000, he had a portfolio of approximately $1,000,000 - much more than he had ever dreamed of having.

At the age of 65, he had to take mandatory retirement from his company and start receiving income from his union pension plan. In addition to this pension plan, he also started to receive social security benefits and had a rental property that produced $18,000 of annual income. Bottom line, he was rolling in the dough and did not even need to tap into his retirement portfolio. The problem was this: he didn't plan on what to do when he retired, so he is unhappy in retirement. He has gained significant weight over the past five years and spends most of his time shuffling around his house with no real purpose.

My point is simple: deciding to retire just because you are 60, 65, 70 or whatever age is not a good enough reason to take such a big step. In fact, I believe many people retire prematurely without taking a look at the "big picture".

There are some people who have thought long and hard about retirement and have a specific plan in mind. Maybe they want to travel or maybe they want to volunteer – no matter the situation, if you have the resources to do whatever you want then by all means do what makes you happy. But, I strongly believe that if you can continue to work, while avoiding the things you do not want to do, you will be much happier in the long run. How can this be? In short, by taking this approach you will be happy about getting up in the morning and doing whatever it is you want to do that day – whether it is a new job, volunteering, a hobby, traveling, participating in sports or even mentoring others.

Unfortunately many people have simply not thought about what they really want to do post – retirement, nor have they determined when they want to stop working. In this case, I usually recommend people continue working, even if they currently have the financial means to retire right away. Why? Well, I have found that continuing to work full-time, or even part-time, can do wonders for your pocketbook, as well as your health. Many clients who have decided to go down this path have told me this is the best thing they have ever done.

My good friend Harvey's father is living proof of the benefits of this "keep working" strategy. At 99, Harvey's father is in remarkably good health and mentally sharp, something he attributes to the fact that he still works. In fact, he recently celebrated his 25th anniversary at a job he started when he went back to work at 72 years of age!

My father's situation was similar. He started his last job at age 59 and retired at 84 with 25 years of service. While he worked, he enjoyed a more active social life, was excited about getting up in the morning, and, more importantly, enjoyed outstanding mental and physical health. However, he kicked himself within six months of retiring because he quit working too soon. How could this be? For my father, it wasn't about money or time or career goals. It was all about the physical energy and mental strength he derived from doing something challenging, rewarding and productive every day. The year before he decided to retire, he appeared to be in his sixties. After retiring, he seemed to have aged 15 years, and by his 85th birthday he looked his actual age.

At the end of the day, retirement is about having the financial freedom to do whatever you want to do, whether it's traveling, volunteering for a worthy cause, or continuing to work. But, it is also a time in your life when you really need to ask yourself: "What do I want to do?" Surprised? You shouldn't be, because with medical advances and improved healthcare, people are living longer than ever. So if you decide to retire at 65 or even 70, there is a good possibility that you could still have 10, 15 or even 20 more productive years. Given this, you need to know what you want to do and then determine whether or not you have the financial means to make it happen.

One way to accomplish this is not to go "cold turkey" when it comes time for retirement, meaning don't quit working all together. Instead, I recommend you evaluate your present work situation and then find ways to eliminate those things you don't enjoy doing. Is this really possible? Of course it is, but it's an option that people readily admit they have not considered. Once again, work doesn't have to be unpleasant. The key is to focus on the quality of the work experience and the satisfaction you derive from it.

A very good friend of mine, Doug McPherson, President of McPherson Enterprises, who specializes in succession planning for owners of construction and aggregate companies, has developed a process called The Meaningful Future Process^{SM}, which helps these owners develop a meaningful future in retirement. The reason is that many business owners have devoted their entire adult life to building their business and now when it comes to retirement they don't know what they want to do. It is important for them to have a meaningful future. Doug asks them, "Do you know where your truck is going?" So, I ask you, do you know where your truck is going? It is important to plan for your retirement, not just financially, but for what you plan to do with your time in retirement so that you also have a meaningful future.

Keep in mind, continuing to work does not mean you have to keep doing what you are presently doing – sometimes that isn't possible, or even desirable. If this is the case, you need to find something in another field that may interest you. For example, I have a client who is a doctor and when it came time for him to hang up his stethoscope, he knew he wanted to keep working, but not in the medical field. He did, however, have an interest in cooking and it just so happened that his daughter was a caterer. Can you guess what he does now? You go it – at 76 years young, he now works part-time as a cook for his daughter's catering business. Needless to say, he loves his new career, mainly because it gets him out of the house and keeps him busy doing something he enjoys.

My point is this: retiring should never mean you quit living, or even working. Retirement should be viewed as another important step in your life – one where you focus your energy and time on doing things you want to do. To make this happen though, you need to have a plan in place and the financial resources to allow for this freedom and flexibility – which is why following a sound strategy of saving, investing and utilizing asset allocation is so critical to your future success.

*****

Tips you can use

If you are interested in continuing to work instead of retiring "cold turkey," here are some things you can do to get yourself started down the right retirement road.

- Draw a line down the middle of a piece of paper. On the right side, write down all the negatives about your job (what you do not like about it). On the left side, jot down everything you like about your job. When you are done, you should have a clearer picture of what kind of job you might consider pursuing instead of retiring. (I learned this strategy from the Strategic Coach program founded by Dan Sullivan. Dan calls it The Retirement Trick®).

Things I like about my job	Things I don't like about my job

- If you are interested in continuing the same kind of work you are doing now, make a "wish list" of the activities or types of jobs you would like to do, whether full-time, part-time or volunteer. Take this list and work with an outside agency to help you find an employer and/or organization that might have opportunities for someone like yourself. If you are looking for paid opportunities, work with an employment agency that helps place permanent or temporary workers. But if you are interested in volunteering in a particular field, many social service organizations maintain updated lists of volunteer opportunities in their particular community. Either way, there are plenty of resources out there for anyone interested in starting a new career path.

CHAPTER TWO

Making Your Future Exciting

If you have decided to retire now, or determined when you might like to, you need to begin planning today.

No matter what your retirement timeline turns out to be, some significant planning is needed. Most importantly, you need to determine what it is you want to do. Do you want to travel? Do you want to volunteer your time? Do you want to work a part-time job? Do you want to go back to school? Whatever your course of action, you need to start laying the foundation now for the things you will be doing down the road when you have more time and resources available.

Simply put, if you do not plan now, you may find yourself waking up each morning with nothing more to look forward to than another day filled with endless hours of television, occasionally broken up by a visit to the refrigerator during commercial breaks, all the while bemoaning the fact that you aren't good enough to join the senior golf tour. Is this really how you want to spend your retirement? I hope not, because so much more is possible if you put some things down on paper and develop a comprehensive plan.

At the age of 65, a leading portfolio manager of a major investment firm retired, but he didn't have any outside interests and/or hobbies to fall back on. So the first Monday of his retirement he asked his wife what they were going to do. She said, "Honey, I don't know what you're going to do, but I have my own plans," and simply left him home alone.

All of us have heard the quote "I married you for better or for worse, but not for lunch." Well, in this case, our retiree didn't take those words to heart, so he sits at home, watches TV and drinks his occasional beer (unfortunately with greater frequency as time goes on). As a result, his health has deteriorated and he no longer has the energy or strength to travel, which is what his wife really loves to do.

This story is a great example of why I believe planning and setting goals is so important. For this reason, I want you to take the time to conduct an exercise that has changed my own life, given it direction, and added some excitement.

Set aside at least an hour to begin the exercise, find a place where you will not be interrupted, and get blank paper and pencil or two. If you are married or have a significant other, it is important to do this exercise with your partner, because he or she will likely play a big part in the process. You are about to draw up a road map for your retirement, as well as for the rest of your life.

Begin by making a list of all the things you want to do in retirement, including some of the things you would like to have accomplished by the end of your life. Write down all of them, including any farfetched, lofty goals you have always wanted to achieve but never thought you could. Put it all out there – daydream a little and visualize yourself fulfilling some of those dreams. They made a movie about this – it's called "The Bucket List" starring Jack Nicholson and Morgan Freeman.

Now, lay out a timeline for achieving these goals. Begin by setting up a long-term timeline with intermediate steps. An example will show you what I mean.

Goals:

1. Break 85 in Golf
2. Get part-time consulting job
3. Volunteer for a charitable organization
4. Travel to all major continents
5. Maintain cholesterol level below 175
6. Take courses with my spouse
7. Hike the Himalayas
8. Learn a new sport
9. Read a book per month

10. Take cooking lessons
11. Take dancing lessons with my spouse
12. Go on a weekend trip each month

Now that you have listed some goals, break each one down into mini-goals. For example, if you shoot 100 in golf, set a time frame to shoot 95, then 90, and finally your goal of 85. Your plan for getting to your goal of 85 might look like this.

Goal: Break 85 in Golf

Step 1:	Goal:
Sign up for golf lessons	Two months from now break 95
Step 2:	Goal:
Practice three times a week	Three months from now break 90
Step 3:	Goal:
Set up schedule with golf pro	Four months from now break 85
to analyze game	

Achieving the rest of your goals is similar. Set time lines for completion of intermediate steps toward fulfillment of your goals. For example, if you want to hike the Himalayas, your steps might include:

1. Search on the internet for commercial trekkers in the Himalayas. You would assign yourself a timeline for collecting information. Then,
2. Determine the cost for you and your spouse. If the cost is too high, set your timeline for taking the trip in a year or two and put the monies aside each month. If the trip costs $12,000, set aside $500 per month in a separate vacation account so the funds are available when you need them.

The key is to plan. With travel costs within the reach of most of us, economical trips are available to almost any place in the world. You can actually go to the places you have always dreamed of visiting.

Keep in mind that the goals you initially establish are not necessarily set in stone. You may wish to go back and change some of the things on your original list as circumstances dictate. Maybe your financial situation changes or something happens in your life (like a death or illness) that forces you to re-evaluate both your short and long-term goals. Either way, these (or a host of other circumstances) may require you to re-assess your goals and change them accordingly.

The main thing though, is to have some defined goals – goals that reflect what you want to do and where you want to be during your 'golden years' – and to do whatever you can in order to move in a positive fashion toward attaining them.

Given all this, our next step – finding a way to pay for it all – is just as important. Looking at the financial aspects of achieving these goals must not be taken lightly. And I can think of no better way to drive this point home than to share another story.

Bob and Nadine have been clients of mine for the past 10 years. When I first met them, they were both successful in their own careers and they had managed to save a significant amount of money. In short, they had accumulated about $1,700,000 in investable assets for their retirement, along with another $7,000,000 in illiquid assets.

Both of them wanted to retire in 2001, but they had never sat down and really discussed what it was they wanted in retirement. Nor had they identified what it was they wanted to have accomplished by the end of their lives.

So, after having decided to transfer their accounts to our firm, they proceeded to go through the planning exercise of making their lists of goals and formulating their timelines for retirement and lifetime achievements. By the end of their first hour of planning, Nadine and Bob were truly excited about what they could realistically accomplish, and more importantly, each had finally realized what was important to the other.

For example, they learned that they were both concerned about the wealth their children would inherit, and how it would impact their lives. Likewise, Nadine learned that Bob had a yearning to sail across the Atlantic, while Bob discovered Nadine wanted to pursue a degree in interior design.

So, by the end of the second hour of planning, they had begun to refine their timelines for achieving their goals, and had initiated the process of defining steps for reaching them. We started by establishing a private family foundation which their children now manage. In fact, their kids are now more interested in the foundation getting the bulk of their parents' inheritance and in doing something worthwhile with those funds than they are in inheriting the money for themselves. Simply put, this has given Bob and Nadine peace of mind that is priceless.

Since that first meeting, Nadine has earned her degree in interior design, and now works part-time for an interior design business. In May of 2005, Bob set sail across the Atlantic, traveling from Spain to the Virgin Islands on a 51-foot sloop.

The bottom line is that by making the commitment to plan, to create goal lists, to set up timelines, to define and analyze their own desires and dreams, Bob and Nadine now have a clear picture of what they want to achieve and a timeline and plan for achieving it.

This is what the process is all about and it offers an excellent example of how it can work for you if you are willing to make the effort required.

*****

Tips you can use

Preparing for retirement and realizing the excitement of your dreams depends, in part, on your ability to identify what it is you want to do and accomplish. Having said this, here are several things you can start doing today.

- When people set goals, they tend to underestimate themselves. Don't be afraid to THINK BIG and write down goals that may seem tough to attain.

- After writing down your goals put them in a picture frame and place it in a spot where you will see them every day. This will serve as a constant reminder of what you need to accomplish.

CHAPTER THREE

Determining How Much You Really Need

Now that you've determined what your goals are, it's time to figure out how much money you're going to need to make it all possible. Are you up to the task? I hope so, because this is an important step in any financial planning process.

I believe most people already have a good idea of how much money they spend per month and what kind of income they need to maintain their chosen standard of living. In the case of my clients, the average person has about $1,000,000 set aside for retirement, but is also looking for $7,000 per month in available income. Does the math work? That depends on a number of factors (i.e. expenditures) leading up to their actual time of retirement. What about you? What annual income do you require? If you don't know, now is the time to take a look at what you will need and begin the planning process.

A good first step to determine how much money you will need to achieve your lifetime goals is to look at your annual take home income and savings rate. For example, if your present net income is $83,000 and you're able to save $11,000 of that amount, your annual after-tax income requirement is $72,000 – the amount you will need to plan on spending in your retirement years. This amount will need to be adjusted annually for inflation.

However, you need to be generous in your estimate of income needs because it's better to have more income than you need at retirement than to come up short. There are also several financial matters you need to take into consideration when determining your future needs – all of which can either increase your income requirement or decrease your investable assets.

For example, here are some things that can INCREASE the amount of money you will eventually need for retirement:

- Education costs for children and/or grandchildren
- Care needs for aging parents
- Long-term care premiums
- Life insurance premiums for estate planning
- Increased health insurance premiums (if retiring before Medicare kicks in)
- Wedding expenditures (this can be big if you have several daughters!) Jim, my good friend, has four!!!
- Luxury purchases (i.e. second homes, lakeside cabins, boats, RV's, etc.)
- Planned travel (i.e. yearly cruises, trips overseas, etc.)

However, there are also some factors that can REDUCE your future income needs:

- Paying off your home mortgage
- Refinancing your mortgage
- Eligibility for Medicare
- Absence of work related expenses (i.e. clothing, commuting costs, lunches, etc.)
- Working part-time

What does all this mean? Hopefully, it demonstrates that you simply cannot pull a number out of thin air and think it will be right. Determining how much money you will need requires some careful thought and planning. This is why it is helpful to use some type of template to not only assess your overall financial situation, but also to compute the amount of growth needed in order to achieve your retirement goals.

Let's say you have accumulated approximately $1,000,000 in assets which constitutes your "nest egg" (i.e. the amount you intend to use for your retirement). However, you need to insure that major expenses are taken into account and subtracted from the overall figure. In short, this will give you the amount of assets you will be able to invest, in order to produce the retirement income you will need for the rest of your life.

Below is an example of how major expenses need to be viewed. Notice how for each event/expense current estimated costs, number of years until completion and inflation are all used to determine the amount of assets you need today in order to pay for it in the future. I have done the math for you.

How Major Expenses Can Impact Your Retirement Portfolio:

Future Lump Sum Expenses in Retirement

Major Expense Item	*Current Cost*	*# of Pmts*	*Annual Discount Rate*	*Annual Inflation Rate*	*Years until Expense*	*Present Value of Expense*
Wedding for daughter	*$40,000*	*1*	*3.00%*	*5.00%*	*4*	*$43,198*
Vacation Home Deposit	*$30,000*	*1*	*3.00%*	*5.00%*	*1*	*$30,583*
New Boat	*$25,000*	*1*	*3.00%*	*5.00%*	*1*	*$25,485*
New Sports Car	*$60,000*	*1*	*3.00%*	*3.00%*	*0*	*$60,000*
Grandson's College	*$18,000 per year*	*4*	*3.00%*	*5.00%*	*3*	*$84,040*
				Total Needed for Future Expenses		*$243,306*

How to read the above chart:

In the "wedding for daughter" expense example above, this client estimates a wedding expense four years from now which will be paid for in one payment. $40,000 is today's estimated wedding cost. Using a 5% annual inflation rate, the wedding cost would be approximately $48,620 four years from now.

Meanwhile, I used a 3% annual discount rate (estimated interest earned on funds earmarked for the future wedding expense until the funds are used).

We need to determine the amount of TODAY's dollars that need to be earmarked specifically for the future wedding. As you can see in the far right column, $43,198 is the "Present Value of the Expense" meaning this is the amount this client should earmark TODAY to cover the future wedding expense.

According to the above chart, this client would need to earmark approximately $243,306 for all the future expenses listed. Therefore, this amount would not be utilized in any retirement calculations.

Assuming the couple in the above example has $1,000,000 in investable assets, they would need to subtract *$243,306* from this amount leaving *$756,694* in investable assets available for retirement.

The tallying, however, doesn't end here because the next step is taking this adjusted "assets available for retirement" figure and adding it as an available source of income. What income will you receive in retirement?

For example, here is a list of retirement income sources potentially available to you:

- Social Security
- Pension income
- Rental income
- Alimony payments
- Deferred compensation
- Trust income
- Annuity income
- Charitable Unitrust income

Now that you've determined how much net income is necessary for retirement (major expenses in the chart), you need to determine the gross amount of income you will require to satisfy the payment of federal and state income taxes. You will also need to determine the ideal amount, if any, to withdraw from your qualified retirement plans (such as IRAs) to minimize the impact of federal and state income taxes – assuming, of course, that you have rolled over your 401(k) and/or 403(b) plans into an IRA, along with any lump sum payments from your pension or profit sharing plans.

This brings us to a very important question. Where will you live? I mean which state do you plan to reside in? This is significant because the state income tax rate varies from state to state. Your state of residence needs to be taken into account when you project how much spendable income you will have after you have satisfied all of your tax obligations.

State income tax is an income tax that is levied by each individual state. Seven states choose to impose no income tax. These states are Alaska, Florida, Nevada, South Dakota, Texas, Washington and Wyoming. Additionally, New Hampshire and Tennessee limit their state income taxes to include only dividends and interest income. As of May of 2009, the highest rate of state income tax is that of Hawaii, with a maximum rate of 11%. Of those states which impose an income tax, the lowest maximum rate is that of Illinois, which levies a flat tax of 3%. Most states, 34 of them, have a progressive income tax, where the rates rise as the income grows higher. In California, for instance, the rate for a single person begins at 1% at $7,168 in income and rises to 9.3% over $47,055. In 2005, California added a mental health tax of 1% on incomes greater than $1 million, making the marginal income tax rate in that state 10.3% at extreme income ranges.

Let's look at an example: Suppose your joint taxable income is $100,000 in retirement, in addition to paying $17,250 in federal income tax (based on 2010 tax rates), you would pay an additional $6,996 if you were a California state resident. That's significant since that $6,996 would cover the cost of a nice vacation each year.

If this is all confusing, trust me, it isn't as complicated as it may sound, but it is certainly one of many important steps you need to take – and it's all part of the Retirement Success Solution[®2]! I will show you how to do this in the next chapter.

*****

Tips you can use

Financial planning for the future can be a big task, but it is an important one. Given this, consider the following when determining how you might better use, or allocate, your money.

- When considering major lump sum expenses, be sure not to short-change yourself. It's better to plan for something that "might happen" as compared to not planning for it at all. This will give you a better chance of actually obtaining it. For example, you dream of owning a motor home but do not know if you will have the money. It's better to plan on this expense (or a portion of it) now, as opposed to not figuring on it at all. That's why it is so important to list it in the previous table and subtract that cost from the investable assets that will be used in retirement. If you do not allow for major expenses in the beginning of your retirement, when you are first starting to withdraw monies from your retirement assets, you may become very reluctant to or unable to withdraw assets for that major purchase.

- If you feel your list of anticipated lump sum expenses is getting too long or pricey based on your anticipated retirement income, consider cutting back and/or downsizing your expectations. For example, do you need both a boat and lake home? Or is there a way you can plan now for a smaller boat and/or consider purchasing a vacation home in a location where real estate prices aren't as high?

- Be realistic. Don't be afraid to fine-tune your "wish list" and their estimated expenses as adjustments are needed. The success of your financial plan is directly correlated to the accuracy of what is actually being implemented.

CHAPTER FOUR

Retirement Planning
For Special Needs Families

Having a special needs child can be very challenging, especially on and for your retirement. It is very important as you plan for retirement that you also consider the needs of your child, while you are alive and after you've passed on.

First, let's look at it from the standpoint of "while you are here." If you have a special needs child then you are already aware of what that child costs. You have living, medical, recreational, educational, work and tax expenditures. Depending on how old your child is, you could be looking at anywhere from 20 to 50 years of those costs being a reality for you.

Once your child turns 18, you can apply for government benefits. In 2011 the Supplemental Security Income (SSI) payment for an eligible individual was $674 per month. Those payments can help offset some of your costs, but more than likely you will need to plan for an additional $25,000 to $50,000 a year in expenses (depending on the severity of your child's disability). Here are some costs to think about:

Living Expenditures	Medical Expenditures
Housing	Doctor visits
Utilities	Deductible expenses
Clothing	Vision care
Food/essential dietary needs	Dental care
Transportation	Medicines & Scripts
Guardianship	Rehabilitation expenses
Insurance premiums	

So what can you do? Well, from a retirement standpoint, one thing that might help is using a tax-deferred variable annuity. This is not an endorsement for variable annuity products, but in this case we are going to look at a variable annuity as a great solution[3] (please see the Disclosure in the back of the book). Many of the insurance companies have variable annuities with guarantees attached to them. They guarantee an income stream (usually 4% to 7% depending on your age) that neither you nor your spouse can outlive. They also guarantee a certain return on your income benefit value (usually the greater of 4% or whatever the underlying portfolio does). An annuity can provide a steady stream of income for your special needs child. The big advantage though, is that many insurance companies have long term care riders that can be added to your annuity policy for a small cost. If your child does need long term care, the insurance company doubles whatever the income stream is (for example from 5% to 10% a year). It is important to remember that the special needs child should be listed as the annuitant and the Special Needs Trust as the owner of the variable annuity policy. Once you pass on, you can leave the annuity to the Special Needs Trust that you have set up for your child.

Let's take a look at a case study.

George and Ginny Crump are 59 and 58 years old respectively. The Crumps have a net worth of about $1,800,000. They have a son, Lester, who is 32 years old. His annual expenses total $26,000. Lester is mentally disabled and epileptic. However, he is fairly high functioning. He has been able to work and has actually been able to contribute to a 401(k) plan. Lester has saved $20,000 in his retirement plan – a rarity for a special needs child. The Crump's big concerns are:

- What to do with Lester's 401(k)?
- Does Lester qualify for government benefits?
- Long Term Care for Lester
- Ensure that Lester will not be a financial burden to his siblings.

The first thing we did was have the Crumps set up a Special Needs Trust (SNT). You can place assets inside a Special Needs Trust and those assets are not viewed as assets of the special needs child. Then we had to make sure Lester was eligible for government benefits.

A person cannot have more than $2,000 in their name to qualify for SSI. Since Lester had assets in his name in a 401(k) plan, the first thing we did was to file a 401(k) distribution form based on a disability. That way we were able to pull the money out without having to pay a penalty for an early withdrawal. Yes, there were taxes due but Lester was in a very low tax bracket.

With the proceeds, we bought a variable annuity[3] that had a long term care rider attached to it. We designated the owner and beneficiary of the annuity as the Special Needs Trust (SNT) and also named Lester as the annuitant. We also used an additional $250,000 of the Crump's cash to fund the rest of the variable annuity for a total of $270,000.

The variable annuity[3] had a feature that provided for a doubling of the income base in 10 years. The 5% income benefit would be based on this amount. Thus, the Crumps knew they would be able to have an additional $27,000 of annual income for Lester commencing in 10 years. This, combined with the $674 monthly income from government benefits, gives Lester an income stream of over $2,900 per month which he cannot outlive. The income stream was just enough to meet all of his needs.

We needed to ensure that the income stream would have the opportunity to increase to keep up with the rate of inflation. The annuity did provide for an increase in income. We were also able to secure long term care for him with the rider we purchased with the annuity, without having to go through medical underwriting. This was important because if Lester qualified for long term care needs, his income from the variable annuity[3] would double to $54,000 per year. This gave the Crumps additional peace of mind that Lester would not be a financial hardship to their other children and, more importantly, would enable them to have a successful retirement.

What if you are getting ready to retire and you still have a young special needs child? Your own parents may or may not be alive, but for now let's assume they are. You will need to talk with them to find out if they plan on leaving any money to your special needs child. If they do plan on it, then you should make sure the money is left to a Special Needs Trust to benefit your child. Remember, if the child has more than $2,000 in their name, this could disqualify them from receiving their government benefits. Obviously, this could impact your own retirement because without the government benefits, you will have to come up with those additional funds.

The greatest concern of most parents who have a special needs child is, "What is going to happen to my child after I die?" You and your financial planner are going to have to take that into account. As we have discussed, the financial burden can be tremendous. So how do most people ensure that the guardians they name to care for their child will have enough money? We use life insurance to do that. Whether or not you decide to use whole life, variable life or term life insurance is up to you. I recommend using some sort of "permanent" insurance, but if term insurance is all you can afford then by all means use term. Remember, you and your planner are going to have to calculate the projected costs for the remainder of your child's life if anything were to happen to you "tomorrow." Obviously the premiums are going to have to be factored in your overall retirement plan and I am sure the cost of insurance will determine whether you decide to use permanent or term life insurance. Again, I want to remind you NOT to leave any inheritance directly to your child but rather to the Special Needs Trust that you set up for him.

I know many parents are concerned about their other children feeling "left out" of any sort of inheritance. The fact is, you do not have to leave them out at all. You and your attorney can set up the Special Needs Trust so that once your special needs child passes on, your assets will flow to your other children.

Planning for a special needs child during your retirement can be a complicated process. You really should talk with an advisor who specializes in planning for families who have special needs children. You also want to make sure you are working with an attorney that knows the intricacies of a Special Needs Trust. Too many times clients have come to see me and said, "Our attorney did this for us. He says he knows how to write a Special Needs Trust." After reviewing many of these trusts I have found that they are improperly written and would never stand up in court. Since you are reading this book and taking the time to make sure your retirement is well planned out, don't take chances when it comes to setting up a Special Needs Trust. Make sure your attorney is very familiar with Special Needs Trusts because your child's future depends on it.

CHAPTER FIVE

Women
and
Retirement Planning

Women require more careful retirement planning than men. Do I have your attention? Good. If you are a woman, this portion of the book is especially dedicated to you. If you are a man, you likely have a wife, mother, sister, daughter or other lady in your life that you care about. As you read this chapter, I urge you to think of them but also think of yourself as a possible future widower.

According to the U. S. Administration on Aging, in 2008, 72% of men age 65 and older were married, while only 42% of women age 65 and older were married. In 2008 there were over four times as many widows (8.8 million) as widowers (2.2 million). This somewhat illustrates the ratio of women to men in that age group.

I recently read the phrase, "A Man is not a Financial Plan." How true this statement is.

Women face special challenges when planning for retirement. This is because their careers are often interrupted to care for children or elderly parents. Women may spend less time in the workforce and earn less money than men in the same age group. As a result, their retirement plan balances, Social Security and pension benefits are often lower. In addition to earning less, women also generally live longer than men. Therefore, women can expect to stretch their limited retirement savings and benefits over their extended life expectancy.

To meet these financial challenges, retirement planning should be a priority.

According to the U.S. Administration on Aging, at age 65, women can expect to live, on average, an additional 19.8 years. In addition, many women will live into their 90s. This means that women should generally plan for a long retirement that will last at least 20 to 30 years. Given the number of widows over 65 years old, women should consider the probability of spending some of those years alone. For married women, the loss of a spouse can mean a significant decrease in retirement income from Social Security or pensions.

Most Financial Planners plot and plan all kinds of cash flow scenarios for couples to live happily ever after. Because no one wants to plan for a time when they may live without their spouse, I often wonder if couples plan to live until they fall gently asleep in each other's arms at age 95. Unfortunately, life is not quite so predictable. Therefore, it is realistic to plan for the probability of outliving your spouse. This includes being prepared to handle all of the arrangements and paperwork that must be dealt with upon death as well as long-term planning for your financial needs.

While today's senior women tend to be more financially savvy than their mother's generation, many still struggle with money issues, especially following the death of a spouse. If you haven't already, be sure to talk with your husband so that you BOTH are familiar with the family finances. This includes understanding your collective sources of income, investment and retirement accounts, insurance coverage as well as their location. You also need to know your centers of influence – your financial planner, accountant, insurance agent, attorney and others. The traumatic time of widowhood is NOT the time to scramble to catch up on your financial knowledge.

What is your excuse for not planning for retirement?

"I'm too busy to plan."

Perhaps you are so wrapped up in balancing responsibilities that you haven't given retirement planning much thought. That's understandable, but if you don't put retirement planning at the top of your to-do list, you risk shortchanging yourself later on. Staying focused on your goal of saving for a comfortable retirement is difficult, but if you put yourself first and plan ahead, it will really pay off in the end.

"My spouse takes care of our finances."

Married or not, it's critical for women to take a proactive role in planning for retirement. Otherwise, you may be forced to scramble to make important financial decisions quickly during a period of crisis. Unfortunately, decisions that are not well thought through often prove costly in the long run. Preparing for retirement with your spouse will help ensure that you're BOTH provided for, and pave the way to a worry-free retirement. Remember to plan for the probability that either of you will live independently at some point during your retirement.

"I'll save more once my children are through college."

Many well-intentioned parents put their own retirement savings on hold while they save for their children's college education. If you do so, you are potentially sacrificing your own financial security. Your children have many options when it comes to financing college— loans, grants, scholarships, and work study programs for example— but there's no such thing as a retirement loan! Why not set a good example for your children by getting your own finances in order before contributing to their college fund?

"I don't know enough about investing."

Your financial planner should integrate educational components to help you further your knowledge about investing and financial planning. Commit to spending just a few minutes each day learning the basics of investing, and you'll become knowledgeable in no time. And remember, you don't have to do it by yourself—your financial planner should be happy to work with you to set retirement goals, help you choose appropriate investments, and continue to educate you along the way.

Whether you are married or not, here are some of the things that you can do to build a more secure retirement for yourself.

Make retirement plans a priority when you consider a job.

- Consider a slightly lower current salary in return for a good retirement plan, and seek out employers who will match part or all of your savings in a contributory plan – an employer-sponsored 401(k) plan for example.

Work as long as you can at the highest salary you can.

- The longer you work, the more you can put away for retirement. The older you are when you retire, the fewer years of retirement income you will have to fund – higher Social Security benefits are an extra bonus for those years of service. If you pay into Social Security for at least 10 years (or if you qualify for Social Security under your husband's work record), you won't have to pay monthly premiums for Medicare hospital insurance when you retire.

Understand the effect of divorce, remarriage and death on Social Security benefits.

- If you were married for at least 10 years and then you divorce, you are entitled to Social Security payments equal to 50% of your ex-spouse's benefits upon your retirement. You will lose that right if you remarry. However, you would then be entitled to collect payments based on your new spouse's Social Security benefits.

- Once you begin receiving Social Security benefits, they continue through your lifetime and terminate upon death. When your spouse dies, you will only have ONE household social security income instead of TWO. As a widow(er), you are entitled to replace your Social Security benefits with your late spouse's benefits as long as you do not remarry before age 60.

Put money away for your retirement on a regular basis.

- Just \$10 to \$20 a week can add up, especially if you begin this practice at a young age. Saving on a regular basis over a long period of time can give you an added pool of funds to rely upon in your retirement years. Many people scold themselves for not implementing a savings plan sooner and feel it is "too late to start saving now." There is no time like the present! Get started today!

Learn about your finances and investments.

- Don't just sign tax returns, insurance policies, and investment account forms, be sure you understand them! Obtain assistance from your financial advisor, tax preparer, insurance agent and others if you need explanations to better understand your situation. Identify your financial assets and debts, and begin to save for your future by paying down debt and budgeting. If you are married, be sure that you and your spouse each understand what you own and what you owe, and when appropriate, use insurance planning for the possibility of death or disability.

Losing a spouse is difficult enough, but adding financial uncertainty can be overwhelming. Too often one spouse has little or no financial or investment experience and has to figure it all out alone: How many accounts do I have? How much are they worth? Will I outlive my money? Can I afford to help my children and grandchildren? How will I ever make sense of all these taxes?

Leaving everything on auto-pilot because "this is what my husband arranged when he was living," is not the solution, nor is making hasty changes. The widow(er) needs an experienced advisor to take a fresh look at your financial situation as a newly independent widow(er) and to help answer, "Am I going to be okay?" and plan for your changed life. This also applies to divorcees and other newly independent individuals.

There is a maze of financial decisions that affect a widow(er)'s future. It is important that you do not navigate this maze on your own, but with the guidance of a trusted advisor. It is important to work with an advisor who will educate you, enabling you to make informed decisions.

Every woman, and man, should plan for the inevitable. Someday one of them WILL end up alone. What if that day were tomorrow? Every couple should have a contingency planning day at least once a year to talk about these things.

Review your estate planning documents (Wills, Trusts and Power of Attorney designations).

- Your estate planning documents ensure that your estate passes to others in accordance with your wishes. Make sure that your Will and Trust properly convey how you want your assets to be distributed and to whom. Will the assets be tied up in a confusing web of Trusts? Is the trustee someone that your spouse and/or children trust?

Discuss final arrangements.

- Many of us still say "if I die" rather than "when I die." Facing death is difficult, but it is the courageous thing to do. If funeral arrangements are discussed and agreed upon, the survivor will feel so much more at ease during the difficult time. I have known many people, both personally and professionally, that let their emotions and grief determine the funeral or memorial arrangements. As a result, they spend much more than intended. Please clearly discuss your preferences and desires with your spouse and your children. When the time comes your loved ones will be very thankful that you did so.

The loss of a spouse is extremely difficult on many levels. Most widow(er)s feel like they are in a fog for the first year. The last thing on your mind will be money, but some issues will need to be addressed. You can make it easier on yourself and plan ahead starting today.

Lastly, we also need to plan on not outliving our assets. While no one thinks about dying, we should at least know what our average life expectancy is. In Appendix 3, see the mortality table for a single life. It also gives you the probability of your dying in a particular year. For example, if you are a 65 year old woman the probability of dying that year is 1.10%. Those are pretty low odds, however, as you get older the probability goes up.

Also in Appendix 4 is the joint life expectancy for ages 63 through 66. I have listed only these ages because to show the mortality of all possibilities would take over 20 pages. You may view these mortality tables by going to http://www.pgcalc.com/pdf/twolife.pdf.

For example, for a male and female couple age 65 their life expectancy is 27.1 years; that's 10 years longer than the life expectancy in the single life expectancy table shown on the previous page. The importance of this is to plan on your retirement assets lasting many years. A retirement income of $100,000 needed today will require $185,394 in 25 years assuming a 2.50% inflation rate.

Note that women outlive men by several years, thus if you are a man reading this book and you have been handling all of the financial affairs of your marriage, please make sure your wife is fully aware of your finances and is capable of managing your financial affairs after you have passed away.

If someone is not comfortable with managing the financial affairs on their own, consider hiring a personal Chief Financial Officer ("CFO"). This person can be in charge of reconciling and paying your monthly bills, providing you with a cash flow statement and an updated net worth report each month. In addition this personal CFO acts as the income tax organizer and can prepare everything your accountant needs to complete your income tax return. He/she could also reconcile your medical bills with the Explanation of Benefits statements provided by your insurance carrier. A personal CFO can work with you to handle part or all of your household bookkeeping and monthly bill paying tasks.

Our widowed clients who have a personal CFO have told us they do not know what they would have done if they did not have the assistance of this person.

CHAPTER SIX

Income Sources, Tax Savings
and
Withdrawal Strategies

Now that you've determined how much you need for retirement, the next critical step is to find a way to make it all happen. This may seem like a daunting task, but it doesn't need to be if you follow a carefully structured plan of attack when it comes to your retirement planning.

Nonetheless, after looking at the income goal you came up with in Chapter 3, you still might be thinking, "How in the world am I going to make this work?" First of all, don't worry – at least not now. Yes, all those lump sum expenses and "big purchases" can add up quickly, but just because the numbers seem intimidating don't shy away from trying to attain your retirement goals.

The key is this: You should be excited about your future! And I want you to realize that thinking this way, infusing that enthusiasm into your savings and planning strategies can help make all those expenses and obligations seem less significant in the long run. Once again, what it takes is careful strategic planning, regardless of how much money you have now, or plan to have in the future.

Having said all this, how and where you get your retirement income after retiring is important. Here's an example of why you need to think carefully about this.

A client, who was a sheet metal worker, retired when he was only 60% vested in his company's retirement plan. He wasn't forced to retire due to health or age reasons, and he could have worked longer, but he just thought it was time to be done – he had it in his mind that he wanted to retire at a certain age and didn't want to budge from that.

I am all for people making a plan and sticking to it, but in this case, he could have made his retirement much more comfortable if he had waited a bit longer. How so? By waiting just two more years before retiring, he would have been 100% vested at retirement and benefited from $1,400 more income per month for the rest of this life!

Just think what you could do with an extra $1,400 per month! Think of how many more trips you could take while retired, or consider how that money could be applied to any number of "dream purchases." Bottom line, money like that can add up to a significant amount over several years. Moreover, this story demonstrates how overlooking key details and variables can cost you dearly in the long run.

Let's now talk about your options if your retirement plan includes a choice of pension options. These might include a pension for your life, or your life and your spouse's life. This is commonly called a joint and survivor annuity or pension.

What you need to decide is whether to take the larger life-only annuity, or a reduced annuity to last for your life and your spouse's life. Let's look at an example.

Bob Smith is 65 and worked for XYZ Corporation for the past 25 years. Upon retirement, he is eligible for a $48,000 per year life annuity on his single life, meaning he will receive $48,000 annual income until he dies. If his wife survives him, she will not receive any income at all. The other option is for Bob to elect to receive a $36,000 per year joint and survivor annuity, meaning they will receive $36,000 annual income until they BOTH pass away. This option provides for his wife if she survives him.

What should he consider? Bob wants to protect his wife, but his financial planner wants him to consider the following: In order to provide $36,000 annually to his wife, he would need a lump sum of $600,000 yielding 6% annually.

At his age, a $600,000 Universal Life insurance policy would cost approximately $1,400 per month or $16,800 per year. So in this scenario, he might choose to receive the joint and survivor annuity since, after paying the life insurance premiums, he would net only $31,200 per year.

$ 48,000 life annuity payment
- $ 16,800 life insurance premium
$ 31,200/year versus the $36,000/year with the joint annuity

However, if Bob opted to include the above life insurance policy as part of his financial plan, his wife would receive a lump sum of $600,000 from the life insurance policy upon Bob's death. Let's assume that Bob's wife is 75 years old upon Bob's death. That $600,000 would purchase an immediate annuity providing approximately $5,800 per month or over $69,000 annually, assuming a life expectancy of 12 years for a 75 year female. This is significantly more than Bob and his wife were originally receiving in retirement. Moreover, a good portion of the annuity she purchases is tax free.

Now, suppose Bob is 60 years old, when life insurance premiums are much cheaper than at age 65, and he purchases a life insurance policy in *anticipation* of his retirement at 65. For a 60 year old male in good health the annual premium is approximately $9,600 per year or $800 per month. At retirement he would elect the life only annuity because this gives him $12,000 more income per year in retirement, which easily pays for the cost of his life insurance premium. He also has a surplus of about $200 per month or $2,400 annually.

Of course, Bob must pay federal and state income tax on the additional $12,000 in retirement income. However, he has now provided his wife with a significant lump sum that will benefit her more than the $36,000 annual pension she would have received with the joint and survivor annuity benefit.

The important lesson to be learned is: If you are working for a company that has a defined benefit pension plan and you plan on retiring from this company, know what your retirement options will be so you can plan ahead to determine if purchasing a life insurance policy makes sense. This is very important if you work for the federal or state governments which have defined benefit retirement plans.

So what is your present situation like? Are you totally vested in a company pension plan or are you ready to retire early? If not fully vested, are you taking part in other retirement savings offerings available to you? It is important to answer these questions and take a close look at the income sources you expect to have in the future – just like you did with your anticipated expenses in Chapter 3.

Here are some income sources many people rely upon during retirement, some of which were mentioned in Chapter 3:

- Social Security
- Pension plans
- Rental income
- Trust income (Usually set up by a parent or grandparent)
- Deferred compensation (Identify if there are any conditions attached to you receiving the income)
- Life insurance policies (Do you really need the coverage if you provide no income benefit to your family? Consider cashing in the policy, or better yet, see an agent who can get you a life settlement which allows you to sell your policy to an organization that will give you more than the cash surrender value of that policy[5].) Please see the disclosure in the back of the book
- Annuity income

The above sources are possible income streams during retirement. Now, let's list the various asset sources that can be used to generate additional income in retirement:

- 401(k) plans
- Individual Retirement Accounts (IRAs)
- SEP IRAs
- Uni-K Plans
- 403(b) plans (Normally offered through non-profit organizations)
- 457 plans (Deferred compensation plans offered through non-profit organizations)
- Money market and savings accounts

- Individual stocks and bonds
- Certificates of Deposit (CD's)
- Deferred compensation plans
- Stock option plans
- Investment real estate
- Mutual funds[4] (please see the disclosure in the back of the book)
- Home equity

Granted, some of these options – like deferred compensation plans and stock options – are not available to everyone. But they are examples of asset sources that people sometimes fail to take into account when planning for their future.

The key is to make sure you've made an accurate assessment of your ENTIRE portfolio before leaping into retirement. To do this, I recommend you prepare a detailed financial statement and update it at the end of each year. Make sure that all assets to be used for retirement are clearly identified. Obviously, there's much more to retirement than sitting back and waiting for your social security and pension checks to come in!

As I've already pointed out, effectively managing your retirement income and assets takes thoughtful planning. In order to achieve all the goals you outlined in Chapter 2, you should make sure you're maximizing the full potential of your assets. And the only way to do this is to take a long-term, strategic approach to tap into your retirement sources.

Two of the most important things to consider are how much to withdraw from your qualified (retirement) assets and how much to withdraw from your non-qualified (personal or non-retirement) assets in order to minimize your federal and state income tax liability. Below is an example of what I mean by this.

For the purposes of this exercise, let's assume that you are a couple who files a joint tax return and is currently receiving the following annual income:

$20,000	Social Security Income
$21,000	Pension & Rental Income
$41,000	**Total Annual Income**

Now look at the following table for a couple filing a joint tax return in the year 2010:

Tax Rate Schedule – Married Filing Jointly

Tax Rate	From	To
10%	$0.00	$16,750
15%	$16,751	$68,000
25%	$68,001	$137,300
28%	$137,301	$209,250
33%	$209,251	$373,650
35%	$373,651	And above

For example, if you have $20,000 coming to you from social security and have another $21,000 coming from a company pension plan and rental income, how much should you be withdrawing from qualified plan assets such as 401(k)'s or IRAs? How much should you be withdrawing from your personal investments? The answer will result in a considerably lower federal and state income tax obligation than simply withdrawing the total amount you desire from your qualified retirement assets.

Ideally, you would want to keep your taxable income at $68,000 or less because the federal tax on $68,000 annual income is only 15%. However, every dollar of taxable income above $68,000 is taxed at 25% (or higher if your taxable income falls within the upper tax brackets).

I have included a template in the appendix that explains my point, as well as a worksheet for you to use to compute the ideal withdrawal amount from your retirement account (401(k) or IRA) and non-qualified (personal) investments.

Let's assume that our retired couple, who has approximately $1,000,000 in IRA assets and an additional $500,000 in personal investments, would like to receive $100,000 in net spendable income per year during their retirement years. They receive $20,000 annually from social security (of which 85% is taxable), $11,000 per year in rental income, and $10,000 annually from a small pension plan.

Given this, how much should they withdraw from their IRA, and how much should they withdraw from their personal investments? This step requires the tax calculation below. Take your time and be patient through this exercise as it will lead to the answer: What is the ideal IRA distribution amount? And what amount should be withdrawn from personal investment accounts?

Below is an example of how to determine what annual gross income can be earned while staying in the 15% tax bracket:

$ 68,000	Beginning of 25% tax bracket
$ 7,300	Add 2 personal exemptions @ $3,650 each
$ 12,000	Add mortage interest
$ 4,000	Add real estate taxes
$ 6,200	Add property taxes
$ 1,150	Add charitable giving
$ 3,148	Add state inc. taxes @ 4.63% for sample CO resident
$ 101,798	Ideal Gross Income (to remain in 15% tax bracket)

The $101,798 represents how much taxable income our retired couple can receive AND remain in the 15% tax bracket with the above itemized deductions.

(Note: If you have taxable income of $101,798 with the itemized deductions listed above, your taxable income after deductions will be $68,000. This is ideal because this is the point at which you go from the 15% tax bracket up to the 25% tax bracket).

Now let's subtract, from the $101,798 of income above, the amount of taxable income they will be receiving. The first source of taxable income is social security and it is important to remember that 85% of this is taxable. Once again, other sources of taxable income during retirement may include:

- Pension income

- Rental income
- Trust income
- Deferred compensation
- Annuity income
- Part-time income, consulting and/or other 1099 income

Now let's see what *taxable* income this couple has:

$	17,000	Taxable Social Security Income
$	10,000	Taxable Pension Income
$	11,000	Taxable Rental Income
$	38,000	Total Annual Taxable Income

Subtracting $38,000 of taxable income from $101,798 of the adjusted gross income amount calculated above leaves $63,798, which is the ideal amount to withdraw from your IRA. Any other income needed should be withdrawn from personal investments because it will not be taxed as ordinary income. However, if you withdraw more than $63,798 from your IRA, you will be taxed at least 25% on the excess, plus the percentage that corresponds with whatever state tax bracket you might fall under at the time. It is important to point out that you should limit the withdrawals from your IRA to 6% annually. Why is this? This has to do with avoiding the depletion of your accounts. In Chapter 9 of this book we will cover this topic. See Chapter 9 for a detailed response to this frequently asked question.

In the above scenario, the annual adjusted gross income for our couple would be the sum of:

$	63,798	Ideal IRA Distribution
$	17,000	Taxable Social Security Income
$	10,000	Taxable Pension Income
$	11,000	Taxable Rental Income
$	101,798	Adjusted Gross Income

Subtracting their itemized deductions (calculated earlier in this chapter), plus $7,300 for personal exemptions results in:

$	101,798	Adjusted Gross Income
$	(33,798)	Itemized Deductions plus Personal Exemptions
$	68,000	Taxable Income

The resulting federal income tax on $68,000 would be $9,362, plus state income tax. We will use Colorado state income tax here of 4.63% or $3,148, for a total tax obligation of:

$	9,362	Fed. Income Tax ($16,750 @ 10% + $51,250 @ 15%)
$	3,148	State Income Tax ($68,000 @ 4.63%)
$	12,510	Total Fed. & State Inc. Tax on Taxable Inc. of $68,000

Thus, for our couple who wanted $100,000 of spendable income, they will need to have a total income of:

$	100,000	Spendable Income Goal
$	12,510	Federal & State Income Tax Obligation
$	112,510	Total Gross Income Required

*(If you are using our Retirement Funding Analysis software on our web site this is the **gross** amount that you should enter under "Annual Income Desired". Obviously, you will use your own figures but you should enter the gross amount that includes the estimated federal and state income taxes you expect to pay plus the amount of spendable income you desire).*

$	20,000	Social Security Income
$	10,000	Pension Income
$	11,000	Rental Income
$	63,798	Ideal IRA Distribution
$	7,712	Withdrawal from Personal Investments - Tax Exempt Income
$	**112,510**	**Total Gross Income**
$	12,510	Less Federal & State Income Taxes
$	**100,000**	**Total Net Spendable Income**

Does all this make sense? If not, don't worry, because seeking out the assistance of an experienced financial planner will help clarify these steps and strategies. Nonetheless, these questions and more need to be carefully considered and become an integral part of your overall planning process, which is why it is important to fully understand what income sources you have at your disposal.

I encourage you to make a "master list" of all your income sources and identify what value (dollar wise) each of them has currently, as well as what you anticipate they will be worth in the future – ballpark figures will do for now. The important point is to take the time to identify these future income sources and become very familiar with what they are, how they work and any rules they have regarding distributions.

*****

Tips you can use

Keeping track of, and safeguarding, your retirement assets is important. Here are some tips you can use to make sure you are properly managing your money:

- Anyone who owns IRAs, mutual funds, individual stocks, and other investments knows how many forms and statements can be generated. However, these documents are important, so keeping them all in one place – where they can be easily accessed and reviewed – is important. Make sure you keep a complete list of your investments – with company names, account numbers and contact information – in a separate, safe location (i.e., a safe deposit box, an office, a relative, etc.). If your home is damaged by fire or flood or any other calamity, having this information safely tucked away will save you a lot of headaches, especially if you don't have any statements or documents indicating your current account balances.

- I also recommend you compile a list of all your assets and be sure to include the location of important papers such as your Will, Deeds on real estate or owned insurance policies. Advise a child, family member, or trusted friend where this list is kept so that it may be accessed in the event of an emergency.

- Don't get sucked into the time consuming trap of checking on your accounts all the time. I know it's tempting to check the stock tables in the paper or watch the pundits on television, but you have better things to do in retirement than worry about what the market is doing every second of the day. You should certainly be familiar with your accounts and pay attention to what's going on in the news, but fine-tuning or adjusting your portfolio isn't needed every day. Watching your account on a daily basis can cause emotional trading, which can result in selling low and buying high. This is exactly what you want to avoid!

- Adding some "extra income" to your portfolio can make a big difference in the things you can afford to do during retirement. Having said this, work with a financial planner to see if working a part-time job might be a good fit for you. Keep in mind, working part-time not only provides more income but also gives you something positive and worthwhile to focus on, as opposed to sitting around your home wondering what you are going to do next. My son-in-law's father works at the local golf course part-time. In addition to making a few extra bucks and meeting new friends, he gets free golf – nothing wrong with that! An extra $10,000 of income is the equivalent of having an extra $200,000 in your investment account and earning 5% on that amount.

- While actively setting aside and saving money for retirement is important, maintaining this habit, after you retire, is also beneficial. Think about it – no one knows for sure how long they are going to live, therefore, a long-range approach to savings is always recommended. Whether you are planning for retirement or already enjoying it, setting aside money each month in interest and/or dividend income generating accounts is a "good habit" to develop and maintain.

CHAPTER SEVEN

Tax Strategies
and
Tax Law Changes Worth Noting

Like the old adage says, there are two certainties in life – death and taxes. We won't talk about death here, but taxes are certainly something we need to discuss because they can have a tremendous impact on your retirement portfolio if you don't plan properly.

In short, you need to take the necessary steps to integrate your retirement planning and tax planning in order to make sure your tax liabilities are fully minimized. For example, what investment vehicles are you using right now to save for retirement? Are these offering you a tax advantage? If so, great, but what kind of tax obligations will they create once you retire and start withdrawing money?

These are the types of questions you must ask yourself as you start laying the groundwork for retirement. This includes determining where you will be getting your income from once your retirement journey begins.

For example, I once worked with a couple that was already retired, but were convinced they were paying too much money toward their tax obligations each year. Money wasn't much of an issue for them, but they did need quite a bit of monthly income, given the lifestyle they wanted to live. Finding ways to cut their tax liabilities would be helpful over the long-term. So with some minor adjustments I was able to show them how they could dramatically reduce their taxes – from $80,000 to around $11,000!

How is this possible? It was just a matter of showing them how they were withdrawing income from the wrong accounts. They were taking distributions from their retirement accounts, which are taxed at a higher rate compared to non-retirement account withdrawals. I advised this couple to begin taking income from their well-funded personal accounts, which allowed them to maintain their lifestyle AND significantly reduced their tax liability.

I cannot tell you how many times I have seen people caught in tax-related situations like this, where too much money is being paid to satisfy tax obligations. Keep in mind that taxes cannot be avoided totally, despite what some experts may tell you. There are, however, steps you can take to minimize the taxes you pay over the long term, even in retirement.

There are legitimate tax strategies for everyone, regardless what your situation or income might be. And just like the process of saving money for retirement, there's almost always a way to make improvements toward getting the results you are looking for – you just have to have the creativity and will power to do it. That is why it's important to work with a proactive financial planner and/or an accountant who can advise you on steps that can be taken to reduce your tax obligations.

For what it's worth, here are 10 or more tax and investment strategies you might want to consider:

1. Now that the capital gains tax has been reduced to 15%, I do not recommend purchasing a variable annuity[3] outside of a qualified (retirement) plan, unless it has some sort of lifetime income provision. Why? Because if you withdraw monies from a variable annuity, the gain on the annuity is taxed as ordinary income. On the other hand, if you purchase a tax managed mutual fund, the gain on the withdrawal will be taxed at the capital gains tax rate, if the fund is held for over one year, which is currently a lower tax rate than the gain on a variable annuity. There are, however, some variable annuities that treat some of their withdrawals as a return of capital and thus a portion is non-

taxed. These companies have received a private letter ruling from the IRS to this effect.

The table below shows the difference in tax after 10 years, assuming a 6% growth rate. The tax on the tax managed mutual fund is $2,438 less than the tax on the non-retirement variable annuity.

Assumptions:

Federal Tax Bracket	31%	Capital Gains Tax Rate	15%
Annual Growth Rate	6%	Annual Growth Rate	6%

Non-Retirement Variable Annuity:		**Tax Managed Mutual Fund:**	
Initial Investment	$ 100,000	Initial Investment	$ 100,000
Value 10 years later	$ 179,085	Value 10 years later	$ 179,085
Withdrawal	$ 10,000	Withdrawal	$ 10,000
Federal tax @ 31% (on the $10,000)	$ 3,100	Capital Gain	$ 4,416
		Federal Tax @ 15% (on capital gain)	$ 662
		Tax Savings	$ 2,438

2. Closed-end funds (CEFs) are professionally managed investment companies that offer investors an array of benefits unique in the investment world. While often compared to traditional open-end mutual funds, closed-end funds have many distinguishing features.

CEF shares are listed on securities exchanges and bought and sold in the open market. They typically trade in relation to, but independent of, their underlying net asset values (NAVs). Intra-day trading allows investors to purchase and sell shares of closed-end funds just like the shares of other publicly traded securities. In addition, when shares of closed-end funds trade at prices below their underlying NAVs (at a discount), investors have the opportunity to enhance the return on the investment by making bargain purchases.

Opportunity to Buy at a Discount – When closed-end funds can be bought at a discount to NAV, investors are buying a dollar's worth of assets for less than a dollar. This can be attractive for two reasons:

> In income-oriented funds, the yield will be higher when it is calculated on actual dollars invested at a discount, compared to the Net Asset Value. For example, suppose a fund has a NAV of $20 per share, market price of $18 per share and generates income of $1 per year. The yield based on NAV is 5% ($1 divided by $20). If you bought a mutual fund at NAV, this is the yield you would receive. But, in the closed-end fund, the yield based on actual dollars invested is 5.6% ($1 divided by $18).

> If during the holding period of your closed-end fund shares, the discount narrows, the reduction in the discount gives a small boost to the fund's performance when you sell the shares. Using the same example as in the paragraph above, suppose you bought the closed-end fund at a $2 discount to NAV, and several years later you sell it at a $1 discount to NAV. Your capital gain would be the change in NAV over this period plus the $1 reduction in your discount.

You can obtain the net asset value of closed-end bond funds from your broker, who can put in an order to purchase these investments at a 12% – 15% discount. If you're patient, you may be rewarded with a significantly higher return than is currently available. Go to www.closed-endfunds.com to obtain net asset value and premium discount information on all closed-end funds. When I first wrote this book, in the early part of 2008, I did not expect the decline in closed-end funds that occurred in the fall of 2008 and early 2009. I used to recommend closed-end funds if they were selling at discounts between 5% and 10%. However, in the fall of 2008 and early 2009 these discounts widened to as much as 40%. Thus, if a closed-end fund was selling at $10.00 per share and the market declined 20% coupled with a hypothetical 40% discount to its net asset value, your closed-end fund was down approximately 60% in value and you were wondering "what the hell happened?" In the summer and fall of 2009 the discounts came back to more normal levels and many of the closed-end funds came close to selling near the net asset value. I am talking particularly about the closed-end funds that were income producing that kept on producing income even though their values dropped well in excess of 50% in 2008. It is important to know whether a closed-end fund is leveraged or unleveraged prior to investing. A leveraged fund has the potential for more income but definitely has the potential for a greater loss as well. The website www.closed-endfunds.com offers more information. You can determine if the closed-end fund you're considering is leveraged or unleveraged and whether it is selling at a discount or premium to its net asset value.

3. If you did purchase a variable annuity[3] at the peak of the Bear Market and it's now in a loss position, consider cashing in the variable annuity and taking an ordinary income tax loss on the entire amount of the loss. This strategy is especially attractive after January 1, 2010 due to the ability to transfer money from a traditional IRA to a Roth IRA. It is beyond the scope of this book to positively recommend converting funds from an IRA to a Roth IRA because there are many tax factors to consider. You should definitely speak with your financial planner and tax accountant to

determine if a Roth IRA conversion is right for you. Keep in mind that assets transferred from a traditional IRA to a Roth IRA are taxed as ordinary income and can result in a significant tax liability. However, if you do realize an ordinary income loss in your variable annuity, I strongly recommend that you transfer the amount equal to the variable annuity loss from your traditional IRA and convert it to a Roth IRA. Many of the new variable annuities have better income guarantees than the older annuities so it may be advantageous to make the switch. Recommendation – have your accountant or a financial planner who is knowledgeable about variable annuities conduct an analysis. If you ask a variable annuity salesperson to do the analysis, they may not be totally objective because they receive a commission if you buy the variable annuity through them. Please see the disclosure on variable annuities in the Disclosures section of this book[3].

4. Contribute $3,050 if you are single, or $6,150 if you have a family, of your personal assets to a Health Savings Plan each year, IF your health insurance deductible is over $1,200 for an individual or $2,400 for a family. These numbers can be increased by $1,000 if you are over 55 years old. The contribution is 100% tax deductible, will grow tax free, and the assets will come out tax free as long as they are used to pay for medical expenses. Trust me, as you get older you will have medical expenses!

5. If you are considering going back to school in your retirement, set up a Section 529 College Savings Plan for you and your spouse. Contributions are not usually tax deductible - you should check with your state. Contributions to 529 plans grow tax free and then distributions come out tax free for college-related expenses. Withdrawals for non-college expenses can be subject to federal and state income taxes plus a 10% tax penalty. This is

also a great way to set aside educational funding gifts for grandchildren.

6. If you are selling appreciated real estate property that has been depreciated, consider transferring the asset to a Charitable Remainder Unitrust before selling the property. You will avoid the recapture, which is taxed at 25%, and the capital gains tax. You will also receive a tax deduction that is based on your age and the percentage annual withdrawal you will be taking. Consult your tax advisor and attorney regarding these trusts. You should also consider doing a 1031 exchange into another income producing property managed by one of the many real estate investment trusts. We will discuss this later in the book.

7. If you do not need your existing Whole Life, Universal or Variable Life insurance policy, consider getting a bid from a Life Settlement Company[5] before cashing it in. They could offer you considerably more for your life insurance policy than your present insurance carrier. Please read the SEC disclosure on Life Settlements in the Disclosures section.

8. If you are thinking of buying an immediate annuity from an insurance company, consider purchasing a charitable gift annuity from a charitable institution. You could realize a substantial tax deduction that you would otherwise not receive from the insurance company. A charitable gift annuity is a contract, not a "Trust", under which a charity agrees to pay a fixed amount of money to one or two individuals for their lifetime, in return for a transfer of cash, marketable securities or other assets – a gift.

The person who receives payments is called an "annuitant" or "beneficiary". The payments are fixed, unchanged, for the term of the contract. A portion of the payments are considered to be a partial tax-free return of the donor's gift, which is spread in equal payments over the life expectancy of the annuitant(s).

The contributed property, the gift, given irrevocably, becomes a part of the charity's assets, and the payments to the donor are a general obligation of the charity. The annuity is backed by the charity's entire assets, not solely by the property contributed. Fixed annuity payments continue for the life/lives of the annuitant(s).

Another advantage of the charitable gift annuity can be realized by gifting appreciated stock to the charity. You do not sell the stock. This allows you to avoid the resulting capital gains tax which would diminish the proceeds you would have otherwise given to the charitable organization. Let's look at an example:

Assumptions:

Amount Invested in Gift Annuity	$ 100,000
Age of Donor	65
Charitable Deduction	$ 31,900
Tax Savings @ 30%	$ 9,570
Capital Gain on property contributed	$ 50,000
Federal Capital Gain Tax @ 15%	$ 7,500

In this example, purchasing a gift annuity from a charity versus a life insurance company saves $9,570 from the charitable deduction and an additional $7,500 from not having to pay the federal and state capital gains tax on the sale of the stock for a total savings of $17,070. That, ladies and gentlemen, is some serious savings!

9. If you are self-employed and have no employees, establish a Uni-K Retirement Plan. This could allow you to deduct a greater amount than a SEP IRA. For example, if you are making $100,000, you can contribute $22,000 plus an additional $18,587

for a total contribution of $40,587 versus only an $18,587 contribution for a SEP IRA. Go to the following website: http://us.pioneerinvestmetns.com and click on Uni-K calculator to get a comparison of retirement contributions for various retirement plans. Work with your financial planner and accountant to determine which retirement plan is most beneficial for you.

10. If you are self-employed, have no employees and have 1099 income in excess of $200,000, consider setting up a Defined Benefit Plan. If you are over 50 years old, you may be able to shelter over $100,000, or 50% of your income, by utilizing a Defined Benefit Plan. In short, it offers a great way to build a sizeable pension in a few years.

One of the best tax strategies for anyone is fully funding a qualified plan, like a 401(k), an IRA or other retirement plan. Given this, you should max out your contributions to these types of plans because they offer the best defense, both short-term and long-term, against taxes. Off-the-wall, risky strategies don't need to be used, nor do you need to stop contributing to non-qualified assets like savings accounts, money markets, and/or stocks. The key is to make sure you are maximizing your contribution to your qualified plan(s).

It is important that you not overlook how taxes impact other aspects of your retirement portfolio. For instance, when selling individual stocks and/or shares of mutual funds, how will that impact your tax liability? Should you cash out now and absorb the taxes prior to retiring, or should you hold on to these assets and use them at a later date? These are the types of questions that, with the help of your financial planner or accountant, you need to address now.

Along the same lines, you need to determine what role social security will play in your retirement plans. Keep in mind, 85% of your social security benefits are taxable. Figuring out how you might dampen this tax liability and/or compensate for this obligation using other income sources is important, especially if social security payments will make up a good chunk of your retirement income each month.

In the end, it is all about finding the right formula for you – one that factors in all your income sources, puts you in a tax bracket that works best for you, and keeps all of your goals in mind.

I have already touched on it briefly, but one of the best strategies in tax and retirement planning is the use of Charitable Remainder Unitrusts. While I could write an entire book on this subject, an example would best illustrate their benefits.

In a Charitable Remainder Unitrust, appreciated assets are transferred into the Unitrust and then sold. Because the assets are in a Charitable Remainder Unitrust, there is no taxable capital gain on the sale of the assets. The taxes that would have owed on the sale of the asset are avoided.

When the Charitable Remainder Unitrust is set up, the Grantor(s) set what percentage income they want to receive from the Unitrust, which usually ranges from 5% to 10%. There are limits on the amount that can be withdrawn. The older you are when the Unitrust is established, the more income you can withdraw from it. Keep in mind though, the withdrawal rate is fixed and cannot be changed once the Unitrust is finalized.

In addition to avoiding the capital gains tax on the gifted assets, the Grantor also receives an income tax deduction based upon the present value of the remaining interest. The income tax deduction is determined by actuarial equations provided by the IRS – hence the confusing nature of the concept! The Grantor actually receives two tax benefits: the first is avoiding the capital gains tax on the gifted assets and the second is the income tax deduction the Grantor receives for the donation of the assets to the Charitable Remainder Unitrust.

Given all this, the withdrawal rate is paid as long as the Grantor is living. Upon his death, the assets are transferred to a charity (or charities) of the donor's choosing as designated in the Unitrust document.

To better demonstrate this, let's look at the table below to see what the total tax benefits to a Grantor would be by transferring $500,000 of appreciated assets with a cost basis of $250,000 to a Charitable Remainder Unitrust. (Note: We will assume this is a 65 year old couple who have elected an 8% annual withdrawal, paid quarterly).

Assumptions:

Federal Capital Gains Tax Rate		15%
Federal Ordinary Income Tax Rate		31%

	No Unitrust	Charitable Unitrust
Sale Price	$ 500,000	$ 500,000
Cost Basis	$ 250,000	$ 250,000
Gain on sale	$ 250,000	No gain on sale
Tax on Sale	$ 37,500	None
Tax Deduction	$ -	$ 150,670 **
Income Tax Savings	$ -	$ 46,708
Net to Invest	$ 462,500	$ 546,708
Difference		$ 84,208

*** The tax deduction is based on the monthly Federal mid-term rate (7520 rate). For this computation it is based on a Federal mid-term rate of 3.40%.**

As you can see, the couple has saved $84,208 in federal income taxes using the Charitable Remainder Unitrust strategy. At a 6% annual return, that is an additional $5,052 of annual income which could pay for a nice vacation each year. In addition, if the couple's estate is sizeable, transferring the assets to the Charitable Remainder Unitrust removes the assets from their estate, thus offering significant estate tax savings.

Many individuals purchase annuities from insurance companies to provide a monthly income – income they cannot outlive, without the risk of investments. An immediate annuity provides monthly income for as long as the annuitant(s) live. If they live long enough to collect income equal to the premium paid for the immediate annuity, they win. If the annuitant(s) die a short time after the immediate annuity commences, the monthly income ceases and the insurance company keeps any remaining principal, meaning, there are no residual funds that pass to the heirs. In this case, the annuitant(s) lose.

A better solution is to consider a gift annuity. In a gift annuity, the annuitant purchases the annuity from a charity, receives a tax deduction based upon the present value of the remaining interest (there's that Greek IRS talk again), and receives a monthly check from the charity. Upon the annuitant's death, the charity, as opposed to the insurance company, retains the money.

Below is an example of what the tax deduction would be for a 65 year old male who invests $100,000 in a gift annuity with a 6% payout:

SUMMARY OF GIFT ANNUITY BENEFITS
<u>**Assumptions:**</u>

Beneficiary Age		65
Principal Donated	$	100,000
Gift Date		3/8/2005
Payout Rate		6%
Payment Schedule		Quarterly
<u>**Benefits:**</u>		
Charitable Deduction	$	33,379
Annuity	$	6,000
Tax-Free Portion	$	3,348
Ordinary Income	$	2,652

IRS Discount Rate is 4.6%

Given this scenario, the entire annuity becomes ordinary income after 19.9 years; and if you are contributing appreciated property, the tax free portion will be reduced by the amount of capital gains reportable each year. If you are contributing short-term gains or other ordinary income property, your deduction may be reduced. In addition, partial payments for the year of the gift will depend on the timing of your gift.

The tax deduction is based on the Federal mid-term rate. The tax deduction for gift annuities has increased above our example here due to low interest rates.

Granted, this may seem complicated, but there are plenty of resources out there to help you. For instance, you can use the Charitable Gift Calculator under Tools & Resources on our website, www.retirementsuccesssolution.com. The Charitable Gift Calculator will allow you to calculate various scenarios applicable to your individual planning opportunities. On our website, you will also find information and other calculators for other charitable giving strategies which are beyond the scope of this book.

*****

Tips you can use

There is more to reducing your tax liabilities then determining your Social Security Income and what income is needed from you qualified plans each month. In fact, ownership of other valuable assets, such as real estate and collectibles, can pose some problems during retirement if not handled correctly. Given this, here are some ideas you might consider to increase your income yet not increase your taxes.

- Selling real estate can trigger a big tax payment. Before selling real estate holdings, create a Charitable Remainder Unitrust, transfer all or a portion of the real estate to the Unitrust and then sell the real estate, avoiding the tax on the gain. And remember, you would also receive a significant tax deduction.

- If you are selling real estate which you have depreciated consider a 1031 exchange. The recapture on depreciated real estate is 25% and a 1031 exchange allows you to defer the tax and invest the proceeds from your sale in a similar real estate property. There are real estate investment companies that have an exchange Real Estate Investment Trust (REIT) that is specifically set up for real estate exchanges. They have a diversified real estate portfolio and usually pay a 6% dividend.

- Where you live can have a significant impact on your taxes. For example, states like Florida, Texas, Alaska, Nevada, Washington, Wyoming and South Dakota have no or very little state income tax. In addition, New Hampshire and Tennessee only tax dividends and interest. Given this, retiring to one of these states can help your bottom line over time.

Lastly, we need to discuss Roth IRAs and the conversion opportunities that are available to all starting in 2010.

The following article on **Roth IRA Conversions - Planning for New Opportunities** was written by Forefield Advisor and is reproduced with their permission.

Roth IRA Conversion – New Opportunities for 2010

With the lure of tax-free distributions, Roth IRAs have become popular retirement savings vehicles since their introduction in 1998. But if you are a high-income taxpayer, chances are you have not been able to participate in the Roth revolution. Well, new rules apply in 2010 that may change all that.

What are the general rules for funding Roth IRAs?

There are three ways to fund a Roth IRA – you can contribute directly, you can convert all or part of a traditional IRA to a Roth IRA, or you can roll funds over from an eligible employer retirement plan (more on this third method later).

In general, you can contribute up to $5,000 to an IRA (traditional, Roth or a combination of both) in 2010. If you're age 50 or older, you can contribute up to $6,000 in 2010. (Note though, that your contributions can't exceed your earned income for the year.)

But your ability to contribute directly to a Roth IRA depends on your income level ("modified adjusted gross income," or MAGI) as shown in the chart below:

If your federal filing status is:	Your 2010 Roth IRA contribution is reduced if your MAGI is:	You can't contribute to a Roth IRA for 2010 if your MAGI is:
Single or head of household	More than $105,000 but less than $120,000	$120,000 or more
Married filing jointly or qualified widow(er)	More than $167,000 but less than $177,000	$177,000 or more
Married filing separately	More than $0 but less than $10,000	$10,000 or more

What's changed?

Prior to 2010, you couldn't convert a traditional IRA to a Roth IRA (or roll over non-Roth funds from an employer plan to a Roth IRA) if your MAGI exceeded $100,000 or you were married and filed separate federal income tax returns.

In 2006, however, President Bush signed the Tax Increase Prevention and Reconciliation Act (TIPRA) into law. TIPRA repealed the $100,000 income limit and marital status restriction, beginning in 2010. What this means is that, regardless of your filing status or how much you earn, you can now convert a traditional IRA to a Roth IRA. (There's one exception--you generally can't convert an inherited IRA to a Roth. Special rules apply to spouse beneficiaries.)

And don't forget your SEP IRAs and SIMPLE IRAs. They can also be converted to Roth IRAs (for SIMPLE IRAs, you'll need to participate in the plan for two years before you convert). You'll need to set up a new SEP/SIMPLE IRA to receive any additional plan contributions after you convert.

What hasn't changed?

TIPRA did not repeal the income limits that may prevent you from making annual Roth contributions. But if your income exceeds these limits, and you want to make annual Roth contributions, there's an easy workaround. You can make nondeductible contributions to a traditional IRA as long as you have earned income at least equal to the contribution, and you haven't yet reached age 70½. You can simply make your annual contribution first to a traditional IRA, and then take advantage of the new liberal conversion rules and convert that traditional IRA to a Roth. There are no limits to the number of Roth conversions you can make. (You'll need to aggregate all of your traditional IRAs when you calculate the taxable portion of the conversion--more on that below.)

Calculating the conversion tax

When you convert a traditional IRA to a Roth IRA, you're taxed as if you received a distribution with one important difference – the 10% early distribution tax doesn't apply, even if you're under age 59 ½. (The IRS may recapture this penalty tax, however, if you make a nonqualified withdrawal from your Roth IRA within five years of your conversion.)

If you've made only nondeductible (after-tax) contributions to your traditional IRA, then only the earnings, and not your own contributions, will be subject to tax at the time you convert the IRA to a Roth. But, if you've made both deductible and nondeductible IRA contributions to your traditional IRA, and you don't plan on converting the entire amount, things get complicated.

That's because under IRS rules, you can't just convert the nondeductible contributions to a Roth and avoid paying tax at conversion. Instead, the amount you convert is deemed to consist of a pro-rata portion of the taxable and nontaxable dollars in the IRA.

For example, assume that your traditional IRA contains $350,000 of taxable (deductible) contributions, $100,000 of taxable earnings, and $50,000 of nontaxable (nondeductible) contributions. You can't convert only the $50,000 nondeductible (nontaxable) contributions to a Roth, and have a tax-free conversion. Instead, you'll need to prorate the taxable and nontaxable portions of the account. So in the example above, 90% ($450,000/$500,000) of each distribution from the IRA in 2010 (including any conversion) will be taxable and 10% will be nontaxable.

You can't escape this result by using separate IRAs. Under IRS rules, you must aggregate all of your traditional IRAs (including SEPs and SIMPLEs) when you calculate the taxable income resulting from a distribution from (or conversion of) any of the IRAs.

Special deferral rule for 2010 conversions only

But even if you have to pay tax at conversion, TIPRA contains more good news – if you made a conversion in 2010, you can take advantage of a special deferral rule that applies only to 2010 conversions. You can report half the income from the conversion on your 2011 tax return and the other half on your 2012 return. Or you can instead elect to report all of the income from the conversion on your 2010 tax return.

For example, if your traditional IRA contained $250,000 of taxable dollars (your deductible contributions and earnings) and you converted the entire amount to a Roth IRA in 2010, you can report half of the resulting income ($125,000) on your 2011 federal tax return, and the other half ($125,000) on your 2012 return. Or you can report the entire $250,000 on your 2010 tax return.

Should you use the special 2010 deferral rule? The answer depends in part on your tax rate in 2010 versus what you think your tax rates will be in 2011 and 2012.

And speaking of employer retirement plans...

You can also roll over non-Roth funds from an employer plan (like a 401(k)) to a Roth IRA). Prior to 2010, the income limits and marital status restrictions also applied to employer plan rollovers to Roth IRAs (commonly referred to as conversions). As with traditional IRA conversions, these restrictions have been removed beginning in 2010, and now anyone can roll over funds from an employer plan to a Roth, regardless of income level or marital status.

Like traditional IRA conversions, the amount you convert will be subject to income tax in the year of conversion (except for any after-tax contributions you've made). But the good news is that the special deferral rule discussed earlier also applies to amounts you roll over from an employer plan to a Roth IRA in 2010. You can report half of the conversion income on your 2011 tax return, and the other half on your 2012 return, or you can elect to report all of the income on your 2010 tax return. And even non-spouse beneficiaries can roll over inherited employer plan funds to a Roth IRA, as long as it's done in a direct (not 60-day) rollover.

Is a Roth conversion right for you?

The answer to this question depends on many factors, including your current and projected future income tax rates, the length of time you can leave the funds in the Roth IRA without taking withdrawals, your state's tax laws, and how you'll pay the income taxes due at the time of the conversion.

And don't forget – if you make a Roth conversion and it turns out not to be advantageous (for example, the value of your investments declines substantially), IRS rules allow you to "undo" the conversion. You generally have until your tax return due date (including extensions) to undo, or "recharacterize" your conversion. For most taxpayers, this means you have until October 15, 2011 to undo a 2010 Roth conversion.

A financial professional can help you decide whether a Roth conversion is right for you, and whether you should take advantage of the special deferral rule for 2010 conversions.

Prepared by Forefield Inc. Copyright 2010 Forefield Inc.

The bottom line is that a detailed income tax analysis is needed to see whether transferring assets from a traditional IRA to a Roth IRA is advantageous to you. If your tax rates are going to be the same in retirement as they were when you were working, my calculations show that it takes in excess of 16 years for the Roth IRA conversion to be advantageous.

However, if you do the Roth IRA conversion in conjunction with planned giving, the charitable deduction can be used to offset a significant portion of the federal and state taxes due from the Roth IRA conversion.

This is especially true if you are contributing to a new Pooled Income Fund established in 2011. In 2011, the assumed yield, which determines the tax deduction for a new Pooled Income Fund, will be 2.80%. This will result in a significantly larger tax deduction than the current tax deduction for a new Pooled Income Fund started in 2010.

For example, if you are 65 and transferring $800,000 from a traditional IRA to a Roth IRA and will spread the taxable conversion event between 2011 and 2012, $400,000 income in each year respectively, as of this writing, you can claim a charitable deduction equal to 50% of your adjusted gross income (AGI). Thus, if your income in 2011 will be $500,000 ($400,000 – half of your 2010 Roth conversion and $100,000 of additional 2011 income), the ideal charitable deduction would be $500,000 of which $250,000 could be used in 2011 with the other $250,000 being carried forward to 2012.

This would require a charitable contribution of $793,034 into a new Pooled Income Fund in 2011. Keep in mind that you receive the income from the Pooled Income Fund for the rest of your life. At your death, the charity that set up the Pooled Income Fund is the beneficiary of those assets. And just as with the Charitable Remainder Unitrust, once the charitable contribution has been made to the Pooled Income Fund those assets are also removed from your estate, thus avoiding a significant amount of estate tax.

Discuss the idea with your financial advisor and tax accountant to see how this strategy can benefit you and your family.

CHAPTER EIGHT

The Retirement Success Solution®

So far we've gone over a number of key elements that hopefully have you thinking about where you are headed in terms of your own retirement planning.

Clearly, planning for retirement isn't as simple as picking a random number which signifies the amount of money you THINK you will need in order to live comfortably. If it was that easy, you wouldn't be reading this book, nor would I have any need to write it – let alone be a financial planner!

As I've tried to point out, the retirement planning process requires a great deal of thought on your part, especially when it comes to identifying and planning for all those things you wish to accomplish during your lifetime. Given this, my partners and I have developed a comprehensive program which helps both individuals and couples do the following: set their retirement and lifestyle goals, develop tax and financial strategies to fit those goals, plan for legacy and health concerns, and provide knowledgeable guidance so they can feel confident about the future. This is what the Retirement Success Solution®2 is all about!

I encourage you to work with your financial planner on the following steps. Some of them you can do on your own. However, unless you are knowledgeable about tax planning, you should work with your planner or accountant on the IRA distribution analysis.

Let's begin.

The process defined

The Retirement Success Solution®2 is a comprehensive, seven-step process that is designed to guide you along the best determined route toward your individual goals so that you can fully enjoy your retirement journey.

Step One – Vision Statement

Before you do any calculations or analysis, a Vision Statement should be created. How do you know what to plan for if you have not clearly indentified your retirement objectives? I cannot stress enough the importance of your Vision Statement. It is imperative to have your advisor and accountant aligned with you regarding your personal and financial goals for a successful retirement.

As you can see below, John and Mary Simpson identify their vision of retirement in terms of monetary and personal goals.

Vision Statement
Of
John & Mary Simpson

We would like to receive $15,000 per month in net spendable income in retirement. It is our basic plan to preserve principal with our investment choices and live off interest and dividends.

We plan to spend most of our time in Colorado during our retirement. We plan to ski, golf, play tennis and bike. We would also like to travel twice a year to various locations around the world.

We look forward to a healthy and long retirement and to seeing our children enjoy life as their families grow.

Step Two – Personal and Financial Statement & Projected Income Statement

Understanding your entire financial picture is the first step to developing a sound financial plan. What is a Personal Financial Statement? Simply put, it is a list of the assets you own and the debts you owe. To begin your Personal Financial Statement, create a list of all your assets and liabilities. Also be sure to label how they are titled (i.e., John Simpson, Mary Simpson, Joint Account, Trust Account, etc.). Your Personal Financial Statement should include liquid assets (i.e., checking and savings accounts), investment accounts, retirement accounts, real estate, personal property, life insurance cash values, business interests, short term liabilities (i.e., credit card debt and auto loans), and long term liabilities (i.e., home mortgage). This will provide you with a snapshot of your net worth, which is the total value of your assets less your total liabilities.

On the next page you will find John & Mary Simpson's Personal Financial Statement. As you can see, they have separated the assets by title which is important for estate planning purposes. John has total assets of $1,593,000 in his name, Mary has total assets of $366,000 in her name, and they have total assets of $1,870,000 owned by John and Mary jointly. Their total assets are $3,829,000. Because they have a $455,000 mortgage, their TOTAL COMBINED NET WORTH is $3,374,000.

NET WORTH INFORMATION

John & Mary Simpson

August 30, 2011	John	Mary	Joint Assets	Total
Liquid Assets:				
Sun Trust Savings	-	-	22,000	22,000
Joint checking	-	-	3,000	3,000
Sub-total	**-**	**-**	**25,000**	**25,000**
Investment Accounts:				
John's Investment Account @ LSM	225,000	-	-	225,000
Mary's Investment Account @ LSM		200,000		200,000
Joint Account @ RBC	-	-	75,000	75,000
Sub-total	**225,000**	**200,000**	**75,000**	**500,000**
Retirement Accounts:				
John's 401(K)	250,000	-		250,000
John's IRA	1,100,000			1,100,000
Mary's IRA	-	150,000		150,000
Sub-total	**1,350,000**	**150,000**	**-**	**1,500,000**
Personal Assets: Furniture, Auto, Boats etc.				
Furniture & Fixtures		-	70,000	70,000
Mary's Car	-	16,000		16,000
John's car	18,000	-		18,000
Sub-total	**18,000**	**16,000**	**70,000**	**104,000**
Real Estate				
Residence		-	1,200,000	1,200,000
Breckenridge Condo	-		500,000	500,000
Sub-total	**-**	**-**	**1,700,000**	**1,700,000**
Liabilities:				
Residential Mortgage			400,000	400,000
Breckenridge Condo			55,000	55,000
Sub-total	**-**	**-**	**455,000**	**455,000**
Total Assets	**1,593,000**	**366,000**	**1,870,000**	**3,829,000**
Total Liabilities	**-**	**-**	**455,000**	**455,000**
Net Assets	**1,593,000**	**366,000**	**1,415,000**	**3,374,000**

Now that we know the net worth let us look at the various income sources. We need to plan how best to utilize our investment assets in conjunction with our current and projected future income to minimize our federal and state income taxes.

We will do this in Step Three.

Step Three – IRA Distribution and Tax Analysis

The integration of tax planning WITH your investment and retirement planning is CRUCIAL! The IRA Distribution and Tax Analysis determines: from which accounts to draw income; how much, if any, should you take from your IRA account; where distributions are taxable; and/or from your non-qualified investments - where withdrawals are not taxable and what allocation of withdrawals will minimize your overall taxable obligation AND meet your income requirements. By identifying the appropriate income and estimated income tax, you will now be able to calculate the optimal gross income to withdraw from your IRA or qualified retirement plan to meet your income needs, but more importantly, minimize your income taxes during retirement.

See the Sample Income Tax and IRA Distribution and Cash Flow Analysis pages, following the next few paragraphs, to follow along with this planning exercise.

In the following example for John and Mary Simpson, you can see that the ideal distribution from their IRA accounts is $29,300 total. Remember, this is the amount that the Simpsons could take from their IRA accounts AND still remain in the 15% federal income tax bracket, which maintains optimum tax efficiency.

However, because the Simpsons indicated an annual net income goal of $180,000 in their Vision Statement, they still need $62,562 in additional income. They will need to withdraw $30,000 from their non-qualified assets and an additional $50,103 from their IRA bringing the total IRA distribution to $79,403, to have total gross annual income of $205,015. This will give them annual net income of $180,000, which meets their income goal. Remember, it is important to work with your advisor and accountant to work through these detailed calculations and analyses.

SAMPLE INCOME TAX ANALYSIS					
[A]	**Step #1 - Calculation of Optimal Gross Income**				
1	Beginning of 25% Tax Bracket			# of Exempt	$ 68,000
2	Add Personal Exemptions	$ 3,650		2	7,300
3	Add Mortgage Interest				20,000
4	Add Real Estate Taxes				2,500
5	Add Personal Property Taxes				3,500
6	Add Charitable Giving				1,000
7	Add Standard Deduction (if applicable)				
8	Add State Income Tax				2,000
9	*Optimal Gross Income with Federal income tax of*			*$ 9,362*	*$ 104,300*

[B]	**Step #2 - Identify Sources of Income**			
1	Taxable Social Security Benefits	$ 30,000 X 85% =	$	25,500
2	Taxable Pension Benefits		$	30,000
3	Taxable Earned Income			
4	Taxable Rental Income			
5	Taxable Interest & Dividends		$	19,500
6	*Total Taxable Income*		*$*	*75,000*

[C]	**Step #3 - Calculate Optimum withdrawal from IRA or Pension Plan**		
1	Optimal Gross Income	$	104,300
2	Total Taxable Income	$	75,000
3	*Optimum withdrawal from IRA or Pension Plan*	*$*	*29,300*

Prepared by: E. Ronald Lara, CFP®
Lara, Shull & May, LLC

CASH FLOW ANALYSIS	
Step #4 - Cash Flow	
Social Security Benefits	$ 30,000
Pension Benefits	$ 30,000
Earned Income	$ -
Rental Income - Depreciable	$ 20,000
Interest & Dividends	$ 19,500
Tax Exempt Income	
Ideal IRA distribution	$ 29,300
Total Income	**$ 128,800**
Federal & State Income Tax	**$ 11,362**
Net Spendable Income	*$ 117,438*

Step #5 - Determine Add'l IRA and Non-Qualified Distributions to Meet Income Needs							
Net Spendable Income Desired	**$ 180,000**						
Add'l spendable income needed	$ 62,562						
Income from non-qualified assets	$ 30,000						
Tax on non-qualified assets	-	**Must be computed on an individual basis**					
Net income from non-qualified assets	$ 30,000						
Federal Tax Bracket		*25%*		*28%*	*33%*		*35%*
Add'l spendable income needed	$ 32,562						
Add'l IRA Distribution needed	$ 50,103		-		-		-
Add'l Federal & State Income Taxes	$ 13,653		-		-		-
Net Additional Income	*$ 36,450*	*$*	*-*	*$ -*	*$ -*		*-*
Add'l amount still needed	$ -	$	-	$ -	$ -		-
Add'l Federal & State Income Taxes	$ 13,653						
Total IRA Distribution	*$ 79,403*						

Summary Cash Flow Analysis	
Gross Income Desired	**$ 205,015**
Federal & State Taxes	$ 25,015
Net spendable income	*$ 180,000*

After conducting our IRA Distribution and Tax Analysis, we have determined that John and Mary Simpson need $205,015 of gross income in order to net $180,000 income, or $15,000 per month. If you recall their Vision Statement, they would like to receive $15,000 per month in net spendable income. Through this step, we have determined how to obtain their desired income in the most tax efficient manner. Now you can start to see how this process starts to come together.

Step Four – Retirement Funding Analysis

Now that you have determined the desired annual gross income needed in retirement and the most tax-efficient method of withdrawal, you now proceed to the Retirement Funding Analysis (RFA) portion of our process.

The Retirement Funding Analysis is used to determine the growth rate needed on your current investments to generate the required income. In other words, what rate of return do John and Mary Simpson need to earn annually on their investments to achieve their $205,015 annual gross income?

Some people have a fixed rate of return in mind that they want to achieve. Some people set 8% as an annual targeted rate of return. If you can achieve your income goals with just 5% annually, why take on the added risk? This is the essence of the Retirement Funding Analysis.

The Retirement Funding Analysis integrates information from your Vision Statement, Personal Financial Statement, Projected Income Statement and your IRA Distribution and Tax Analysis. The idea is to calculate the *growth rate* needed to best obtain *YOUR* retirement goals. This growth rate is *YOUR* personalized growth rate.

Before you begin the Retirement Funding Analysis, you will need to gather some information in order to complete the process. Take time now to gather this information and consider your answers in the following areas:

1. **Desired retirement age**
2. **Gross annual income you want in retirement** – we did this exercise in the previous step.

3. **Retirement assets at death** – the amount you want "left over" for your heirs upon your death.

4. **Estimated annual inflation rate**

5. **Life expectancy** – to what age retirement income must last. Plan on living longer than you think you will. See the Appendix for the mortality tables for both males and females.

6. **Total retirement assets available** – the current value of your 401(k), IRA accounts, and other retirement accounts.

7. **Future annual retirement contributions** – both employee and employer, if applicable.

8. **Personal investment assets** – those that will be used for retirement. Do not include the value of your personal residence or other illiquid assets.

9. **Personal annual savings until retirement** – remember do not include your retirement contributions as we accounted for them above.

10. **Deferred compensation lump sum payments**

11. **Deferred compensation annual benefits** – how long will you receive benefits and how much will you receive each year?

12. **Stock Option details**

13. **Annual Pension income**

14. **Social Security benefits** – for you and your spouse. Include the age at which you will begin receiving Social Security benefits.

15. **Net Rental Income** – after rental-related expenses.

16. **Other sources of income** – i.e., alimony, Trust income, etc.

17. **Any potential inheritances** – and a conservative estimate of when and how much you might receive.

18. **Cost of living increases on Social Security benefits**

19. **Cost of living increases on pension income**

In the simple Retirement Funding Analysis provided, John Simpson, born on April 24, 1950 is 60 years old. John would like to retire in five years. Remember, he would like an annual gross income of $205,015, which we calculated in the IRA Distribution and Income Tax Analysis step earlier in this chapter. John and Mary have accumulated the following investable assets, as listed on their Personal Financial Statement earlier in this chapter:

Various IRA assets:	$	1,250,000
401(k) assets:	$	250,000
Personal Investments:	$	500,000
Total assets		$2,000,000

In addition, the Simpsons will contribute $30,000 annually into John's SEP IRA for the next five years.

They are planning on this retirement withdrawal, $205,015 per year adjusted annually at 2% for inflation, until age 92. They do not intend to invade their principal.

Most advisors, as well as myself, recommend that clients shift their investment portfolio to a more conservative allocation upon retirement. Rather than capital appreciation and growth, income generation and capital preservation become the primary investment objectives. The main goal is to reduce the risk exposure and volatility within the investments during the retirement income phase.

Therefore the Simpsons set their post-retirement growth rate at 5.50%. They still want to achieve their $205,015 annual retirement income goal but need to do so utilizing a conservative investment allocation with a target growth rate that should not surpass 5.50% after retiring. Again, it is important to be more conservative during retirement in order to reduce the risk of declining retirement assets in a bear market.

So what growth rate do John and Mary Simpson need to achieve over the next five years, "pre-retirement", to allow for their $205,015 annual gross income upon retirement?

By completing the Retirement Funding Analysis the Simpsons learned that they need to earn **6.97%** on their investable assets, over the next five "pre-retirement" years. This return, in conjunction with their **5.50%** "post-retirement" growth rate, should enable John and Mary Simpson to achieve their retirement and lifetime goals. See the following output of the Retirement Funding Analysis example.

The complementary Retirement Funding Analysis tool can be accessed at www.retirementsuccesssolution.com under Tools & Resources, click Financial Calculators and click Retirement Funding Analysis. Good Luck.

Now that we have calculated their pre- and post-retirement growth rate goals, 6.97% and 5.50% respectively, we need to ask: How should they invest their funds to target these rates of return?

In Step 5 we will cover asset allocation.

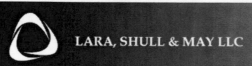

LARA, SHULL & MAY LLC

THE RETIREMENT FUNDING ANALYSIS

PREPARED FOR **John Simpson**   DATE **09/16/2011**

PREPARED BY **E. Ronald Lara CFP**

GENERAL INFORMATION

BIRTHDATE **08/15/1951**   SPOUSE BIRTHDATE **12/22/1952**

AGE YOU PLAN TO RETIRE **65**

POST RETIREMENT GROWTH RATE DESIRED **5%**

FOR RETIREMENT AGES: **65** TO **92**

  ANNUAL RETIREMENT INCOME DESIRED (today's dollars, beforetax) **$205,015**

  Retirement Income Inflation Rate (% increase of Annual Income desired) **2%**

FOR RETIREMENT AGES: **92** TO **92**

  ANNUAL RETIREMENT INCOME DESIRED (today's dollars, beforetax) **$0**

  Retirement Income Inflation Rate (% increase of Annual Income desired) **0%**

FOR RETIREMENT AGES: **92** TO **92**

  ANNUAL RETIREMENT INCOME DESIRED (today's dollars, beforetax) **$0**

  Retirement Income Inflation Rate (% increase of Annual Income desired) **0%**

LIFE EXPECTANCY AGE **92**

RETIREMENT ASSETS AT DEATH (Assets to leave your heirs) **$2,000,001**

RETIREMENT TAX BRACKET

FEDERAL **28.000%**   STATE **4.630%**

RETIREMENT ASSETS

STOCK OPTIONS VALUE $ **0**

CURRENT RETIREMENT ASSETS (401k, IRA, SEP, Pension and profit sharing assets, etc.) **$1,500,000**

ANNUAL RETIREMENT CONTRIBUTIONS (Individual and employer contributions **$30,000**

INDIVIDUAL ASSETS (Liquid assets to be used for retirement, not including personal residence or other non-liquid assets) **$500,000**

ANNUAL SAVINGS (Amount deposited into savings plan per year) **$0**

DEFERRED COMPENSATION BALANCE TO DATE **$0**

ANNUAL DEFERRED COMPENSATION CONTRIBUTIONS **$0**

ONE TIME LUMP CONTRIBUTION **$0**

ONE TIME LUMP CONTRIBUTION AGE **0**

NOTES

RETIREMENT INCOME SOURCES

ANNUAL PENSION INCOME AT RETIREMENT **30,000**

AGE PENSION INCOME BEGINS **65**

ANNUAL SOCIAL SECURITY INCOME **$30,000**

AGE SOCIAL SECURITY INCOME BEGINS **65**

SPOUSE'S ANNUAL SOCIAL SECURITY INCOME **$0**

SPOUSE'S AGE SOCIAL SECURITY INCOME BEGINS **62**

DEFERRED COMPENSATION ANNUAL INCOME **$0**

AGE DEFERRED COMPENSATION BENEFITS END **92**

ANNUAL OTHER INCOME 1 (Rental, royalty income etc.)

   AMOUNT: **$20,000**

   STARTING AGE: **65**

   ENDING AGE: **92**

   INFLATION: **3%**

ANNUAL OTHER INCOME 2

   AMOUNT: **$0**

   STARTING AGE:

   ENDING AGE:

   INFLATION: **%**

NOTES

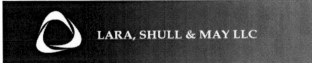

LARA, SHULL & MAY LLC

THE RETIREMENT FUNDING ANALYSIS

COST OF LIVING ADJUSTMENTS

SOCIAL SECURITY COLI (Cost of living adjustments) **2**

PENSION COLI (Cost of living increase, annually) **2%**

NOTES

Based on the information you provided, the growth rate needed to achieve your retirement goals is **6.97%**

See below for your projected retirement assets, per year, based on your calculated investmentgrowth rate and savings rate.

It has been shown that asset allocation—not market timing or stock selection—is the primary determinant of variation in portfolio performance. Most individuals take on too much risk in their investments and thus fail to achieve their goals. In the current economic climate, it is especially important to have the correct asset allocation.

We would like to help you achieve your retirement planning goals. Please contact us for the proper asset allocation based on the above growth rate and your risk tolerance.

PRE-RETIREMENT ACCUMULATION

Age	Annual Contributions	Projected Assets
60	$30,000	$2,169,400
61	$30,000	$2,350,607
62	$30,000	$2,544,445
63	$30,000	$2,751,792
64	$30,000	$2,973,592

The above is by no means a guarantee of future performance. Actual results will vary.

LARA, SHULL & MAY LLC

THE RETIREMENT FUNDING ANALYSIS

RETIREMENT YEARS

Age	Retirement Income Desired	SS Pension Benefits	Deferred Comp. Other Income	Shortfall	Remaining Retirement Assets
65	$226,353	$66,245	$20,000	$140,108	$2,982,164
66	$230,880	$67,570	$20,600	$142,710	$2,988,561
67	$235,498	$68,921	$21,218	$145,359	$2,992,631
68	$240,208	$70,300	$21,855	$148,054	$2,994,209
69	$245,012	$71,706	$22,510	$150,796	$2,993,123
70	$249,912	$73,140	$23,185	$153,587	$2,989,192
71	$254,910	$74,602	$23,881	$156,427	$2,982,225
72	$260,009	$76,095	$24,597	$159,317	$2,972,019
73	$265,209	$77,616	$25,335	$162,257	$2,958,363
74	$270,513	$79,169	$26,095	$165,249	$2,941,033
75	$275,923	$80,752	$26,878	$168,293	$2,919,792
76	$281,442	$82,367	$27,685	$171,390	$2,894,391
77	$287,070	$84,014	$28,515	$174,541	$2,864,570
78	$292,812	$85,695	$29,371	$177,746	$2,830,052
79	$298,668	$87,409	$30,252	$181,008	$2,790,547
80	$304,642	$89,157	$31,159	$184,325	$2,745,749
81	$310,734	$90,940	$32,094	$187,700	$2,695,336
82	$316,949	$92,759	$33,057	$191,133	$2,638,970
83	$323,288	$94,614	$34,049	$194,625	$2,576,293
84	$329,754	$96,506	$35,070	$198,177	$2,506,930
85	$336,349	$98,436	$36,122	$201,790	$2,430,487
86	$343,076	$100,405	$37,206	$205,465	$2,346,546
87	$349,937	$102,413	$38,322	$209,202	$2,254,671
88	$356,936	$104,461	$39,472	$213,003	$2,154,402
89	$364,075	$106,551	$40,656	$216,868	$2,045,254
90	$371,356	$108,682	$41,876	$220,799	$1,926,717
91	$378,783	$110,855	$43,132	$224,796	$1,798,257
92	$0	$113,072	$0	- $113,072	$2,001,242

Disclosure

An Asset Allocation Analysis is a tool that may assist you in determining if you have the right mix of investments for your personal situation. Development of a personalized Asset Allocation Analysis is designed to assist you in positioning your assets based on your financial objectives, time horizons and risk tolerance. The following report is a hypothetical illustration using assumed rates of return that are based on information provided to the advisor from sources we believe to be reliable. Depicted rates of return are not representative of the actual rate of return that will be experienced with any particular insurance or financial product. This illustration is based on the concepts of Modern Portfolio Theory, which states that through diversification you may be able to minimize the effects of investment risks and that gains in one investment class may help offset losses in another. There is no certainty that any investment or strategy will be profitable or successful in achieving your specific investment objectives. The illustration shown should not be considered as a prediction of any investment results.

Principal values of your investments will fluctuate and when redeemed, may be worth more or less than your original investment. Asset allocation does not ensure a profit or protect against losses in a declining market.

Asset mixes presented throughout this analysis are derived using available historical information for each asset class based on the selected index for that class. They are meant only to illustrate the relative experience between asset classes and portfolios. Other asset classes and indices may have characteristics similar or superior to those being analyzed here.

IMPORTANT: The projections or other information generated by AllocationMaster regarding the likelihood of various investment outcomes are hypothetical in nature, do not reflect actual investment results and are not guarantees of future results. The results of this analysis may vary with each use and over time.

Step Five – Asset Allocation Analysis

It is very important to properly allocate your investments to target your growth rate, determined in the Retirement Funding Analysis step above. The Asset Allocation Analysis determines how to invest your money with the highest probability of achieving your growth rate while minimizing the risk in your portfolio. Why take an additional risk for additional return if it is not needed to meet your goals? Too often, investors take on too much risk when it is not necessary. The Asset Allocation Analysis projects future returns and risks utilizing a Monte Carlo simulation along with historical data. You will learn more about Monte Carlo simulation in Chapter 9 - Probability of Success.

The following two pages show the proposed asset allocation recommended to target a 6.97% annual return.

KEEP IN MIND THIS BY NO MEANS IS A GUARANTEE THAT THIS DESIRED GROWTH RATE WILL BE ACHIEVED.

John & Mary Simpson

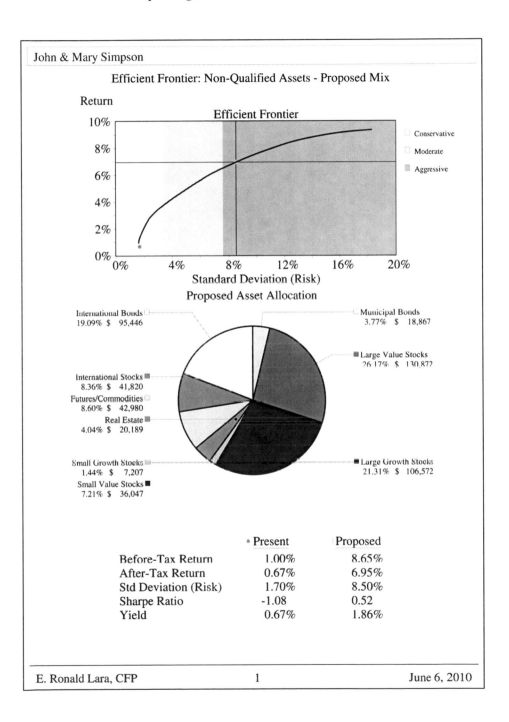

Efficient Frontier: Non-Qualified Assets - Proposed Mix

Return

Efficient Frontier

- Conservative
- Moderate
- Aggressive

Standard Deviation (Risk)

Proposed Asset Allocation

International Bonds
19.09% $ 95,446

Municipal Bonds
3.77% $ 18,867

Large Value Stocks
26.17% $ 130,872

International Stocks
8.36% $ 41,820

Futures/Commodities
8.60% $ 42,980

Real Estate
4.04% $ 20,189

Small Growth Stocks
1.44% $ 7,207

Small Value Stocks
7.21% $ 36,047

Large Growth Stocks
21.31% $ 106,572

	• Present	Proposed
Before-Tax Return	1.00%	8.65%
After-Tax Return	0.67%	6.95%
Std Deviation (Risk)	1.70%	8.50%
Sharpe Ratio	-1.08	0.52
Yield	0.67%	1.86%

E. Ronald Lara, CFP   1   June 6, 2010

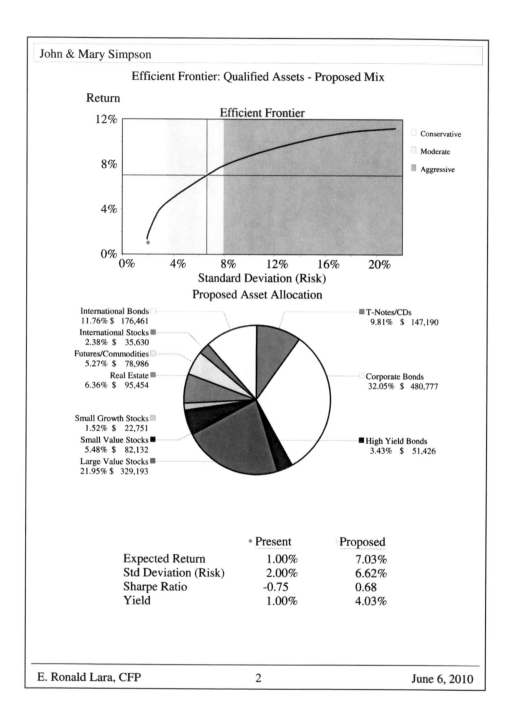

John & Mary Simpson

Efficient Frontier: Qualified Assets - Proposed Mix

Return

Efficient Frontier

- Conservative
- Moderate
- Aggressive

Standard Deviation (Risk)

Proposed Asset Allocation

International Bonds 11.76% $ 176,461
International Stocks 2.38% $ 35,630
Futures/Commodities 5.27% $ 78,986
Real Estate 6.36% $ 95,454
Small Growth Stocks 1.52% $ 22,751
Small Value Stocks 5.48% $ 82,132
Large Value Stocks 21.95% $ 329,193

T-Notes/CDs 9.81% $ 147,190
Corporate Bonds 32.05% $ 480,777
High Yield Bonds 3.43% $ 51,426

	• Present	Proposed
Expected Return	1.00%	7.03%
Std Deviation (Risk)	2.00%	6.62%
Sharpe Ratio	-0.75	0.68
Yield	1.00%	4.03%

Step Six – Investment Policy Statement

The Investment Policy Statement is a statement between you and your financial planner that clearly states your goals and objectives. It indicates how your assets will be allocated to best achieve those objectives. On the following pages is a sample investment policy statement.

Again, it is worth noting that it is CRUCIAL that your advisor understands your goals and is aligned with your vision.

Let me ask you a question. Do you know why you own the investments in your portfolio? Has your advisor or broker discussed goals and objectives with you? The Investment Policy Statement ensures that you and your advisor are on the same page.

John & Mary Simpson

SECTION 1. SUMMARY

The Investment Policy Statement considers the information you have provided about your present and future financial circumstances. It is to document and ensure the long-term adherence to an investment program. It covers the policies, practices and procedures for managing your investment assets.

Plan Title: John & Mary Simpson

Total Assets: $ 2,000,000

Time Horizon: 5 years

Return Objective: 7.44% (pre-tax gross)
                   7.01% (after-tax net)

Client Risk Tolerance: Moderate

Proposed Portfolio Risk Region:
                   Non-Qualified: Aggressive
                   Qualified: Moderate

SECTION 2. OBJECTIVES

These are the main objectives of the investment program. The objectives have been developed in conjunction with a review of your financial resources, financial goals, asset allocation, risk tolerance and time horizon.

1. To take a reasonable amount of investment risk. To maximize return at that risk level.

2. To maintain a prudent diversification of the investment assets.

3. To have the ability to meet the financial goals when each is expected to occur.

4. To minimize potential tax liabilities.

5. To maintain a level of cash reserves in order to meet short-term emergency expenditures.

6. To periodically monitor and revise the portfolio as required.

E. Ronald Lara, CFP

John & Mary Simpson

SECTION 3. TIME HORIZON

This investment program is based on an investment time horizon of at least five years. The investment program does not attempt to consider the active management of short-term investment fluctuations. The asset allocation has been developed as a long-term strategy for the management of your investment assets.

SECTION 4. RISK TOLERANCE

Your ability to tolerate the uncertainties, complexities and volatility inherent in the investment markets has been considered in the development of your investment program. The risk tolerance assessment for your portfolio is shown in the Summary section. This profile was developed in part through the use of a risk profiling questionnaire.

Some of the main factors that influence your risk tolerance assessment are: (1) Your age; (2) Your present financial condition; (3) Your future financial goals; (4) Your discretionary income and its variability; (5) and several other factors. These factors suggest your ability to accept investment risk in order to meet your long-term financial goals.

SECTION 5. EXPECTED PERFORMANCE

The long-term expected rate of return on your portfolio is shown below. It is based on the expected long-term total return for each asset class and its percentage weighting in your portfolio. This is compared against the assumed long-term average rate of inflation (as measured by the Consumer Price Index). The difference between your rate of return and the inflation rate is your real (after-inflation) expected return. Actual performance will vary from these assumed rates. The portfolio return may also be reduced by the deduction of advisory, money management, custodial and transaction fees.

Portfolio Return Objective: 7.44% (pre-tax gross)
                                    7.01% (after-tax net)

Long-Term Inflation Assumption: 2.50%

E. Ronald Lara, CFP

John & Mary Simpson

SECTION 6. HOLDING LIMITS

Your portfolio was developed subject to certain holding limitations. These are limitations on the minimum and maximum percentage investment in each asset class.

Holding Limits

Asset Class	Non-Qualified Assets		Qualified Assets		Annuity Assets	
	Min %	Max %	Min %	Max %	Min %	Max %
Cash Equivalents	0.00%	100.00%	0.00%	100.00%	0.00%	100.00%
T-Notes/CDs	0.00	100.00	0.00	100.00	0.00	100.00
Inter-Term Govt Bond	0.00	100.00	0.00	100.00	0.00	100.00
Long-Term Govt Bond	0.00	100.00	0.00	100.00	0.00	100.00
Municipal Bonds	0.00	100.00	0.00	0.00	0.00	100.00
Corporate Bonds	0.00	100.00	0.00	100.00	0.00	100.00
Mtge Backed Bonds	0.00	100.00	0.00	100.00	0.00	100.00
High Yield Bonds	0.00	100.00	0.00	100.00	0.00	100.00
Large Value Stocks	0.00	100.00	0.00	100.00	0.00	100.00
Large Growth Stocks	0.00	100.00	0.00	100.00	0.00	100.00
Small Value Stocks	0.00	100.00	0.00	100.00	0.00	100.00
Small Growth Stocks	0.00	100.00	0.00	100.00	0.00	100.00
MidCap Stocks	0.00	100.00	0.00	100.00	0.00	100.00
Balanced Funds	0.00	100.00	0.00	100.00	0.00	100.00
Real Estate	0.00	100.00	0.00	100.00	0.00	100.00
Futures/Commodities	0.00	10.00	0.00	10.00	0.00	10.00
International Stocks	0.00	100.00	0.00	100.00	0.00	100.00
International Bonds	0.00	100.00	0.00	100.00	0.00	100.00
Emerging Equities	0.00	10.00	0.00	10.00	0.00	10.00

E. Ronald Lara, CFP

John & Mary Simpson

SECTION 7. ASSET ALLOCATION

Based on your financial resources, financial goals, time horizon, tax status, holding limitations, risk tolerance and expected investment performance a recommended portfolio has been determined. The portfolio balances risk and reward and attempts to achieve the stated objectives of the investment program. The composite asset allocation for your investment program is as shown:

▨	T-Notes/CDs	147,194	7.36
▨	Municipal Bonds	18,868	0.94
☐	Corporate Bonds	480,791	24.04
■	High Yield Bonds	51,428	2.57
■	Large Value Stocks	460,079	23.00
■	Large Growth Stocks	106,575	5.33
■	Small Value Stocks	118,183	5.91
☐	Small Growth Stocks	29,959	1.50
▨	Real Estate	115,647	5.78
▨	Futures/Commodities	121,970	6.10
▨	International Stocks	77,453	3.87
☐	International Bonds	271,915	13.60

SECTION 8. MONITORING AND REVIEW

Investment performance will be monitored and reported to you on a quarterly basis. The investment performance of your investment program shall be compared against the appropriate benchmarks. The investment program will be reviewed at least annually to make sure that it continues to achieve your stated objectives. Since this investment program is long-term in nature, the periodic adjustments made to your investment program should be small.

E. Ronald Lara, CFP

John & Mary Simpson

SECTION 9. REBALANCING

The percentage weighting to each asset class within the investment portfolio will vary. The percentage weighting within each asset class will be allowed to vary within a reasonable range of +/- 5% to 10% depending upon market conditions. When rebalancing is required, investment yield and net cash inflows will be used to meet the strategic asset allocation targets. If cash flow is not sufficient to meet the target allocation for an asset class, we will decide whether to effect transactions in order to rebalance the asset allocation.

SECTION 10. SELECTION CRITERIA

Investment products used to implement the investment program shall be subject to selection criteria. At a minimum, the investment product must be registered, have sufficient historical performance, provide timely compliant quarterly performance, provide necessary details about the firm (personnel, clients, fees, etc.), and strictly adhere to a clearly articulated investment philosophy. Each investment product will be monitored for adherence to your investment policy guidelines, major changes in the product, and comparative performance with similar investment products.

E. Ronald Lara, CFP

John & Mary Simpson

ACCEPTANCE AND ADOPTION:

I (we) have reviewed, approved and adopted this Investment Policy Statement for the investment program prepared with the assistance of E. Ronald Lara, CFP.

Investor's Signature   Date

Investor's Signature   Date

Advisor's Signature   Date

E. Ronald Lara, CFP

Step Seven – Goal Sheet

A Quarterly Goal Sheet should be created that tracks your portfolio's progress relative to your goal. It should show quarterly, year-to-date, and since inception performance of your accounts. It is important to measure your progress relative to **YOUR** goal, as opposed to an index which might have no correlation to your goal.

Are you ahead, behind, or right on track with your goal? The Goal Sheet illustrates the progression of your assets compared to your identified goal. Maybe you are still in the wealth accumulation stage or perhaps you have retired and are taking distributions from your retirement accounts. The Goal Sheet gives you a visual picture of your progress relative to your goal.

Have a look at John and Mary Simpson's Goal Sheet. Using their individual growth rate of 6.97%, the Goal Sheet projects what their assets should be each quarter for the next several years to stay in line with their identified goals. It also shows their portfolio's performance quarterly, year-to-date, and since inception. This is a sample Goal Sheet and does not represent an actual account.

By simply looking at the chart, the Simpsons can see where they are in relation to their goal. With just a quick glance, they can see clearly that they are ahead of their target growth rate of 6.97%. In the sample Goal Sheet, you can see that they have earned 7.56% in their first year. This gives them confidence that they are on the right path and are continuing to make progress toward achieving their goals of enjoying a successful retirement.

I encourage all of you reading this book to have your financial advisor provide you with a Goal Sheet so you can track your assets relative to your goals.

Prepared for: John & Mary Simpson

Goals: 6.97% Yearly
1.70% Quarterly

	Jun-09	Sep-09	Dec-09	Mar-10	Jun-10	Sep-10	Dec-10
Personal Investments	$ 500,000	$ 505,000	$ 512,300	$ 517,575	$ 525,675	-	-
Mary's IRA	$ 150,000	$ 152,000	$ 156,750	$ 167,500	$ 183,450		
John's IRA & 401(k)	$ 1,350,000	$ 1,375,000	$ 1,403,250	$ 1,502,375	$ 1,535,000		
Total Assets	**$ 2,000,000**	**$ 2,032,000**	**$ 2,072,300**	**$ 2,187,450**	**$ 2,244,125**	**$**	**$**
Period Net Deposits and Withdrawals	$ -	$ 7,500	$ 7,500	$ 7,500	$ 7,500		
Total Net Deposits and Withdrawals	$ -	$ 7,500	$ 15,000	$ 22,500	$ 30,000	$	$
Total Dollar Gain/Loss		**$ 24,500**	**$ 57,300**	**$ 164,950**	**$ 214,125**		
Period Performance (adjusted)		1.22%	1.61%	5.18%	2.24%		
Year to Date Performance (adjusted)		1.22%	2.85%	5.18%	7.53%		
Total Tracked Performance (adjusted)		1.22%	2.85%	8.17%	10.60%		

Goal and Performance

Legend:
- Adjusted Goal Value
- Actual Value

These figures are projections only and are not guarantees of future performance. These are planning estimates only. The account values shown herein are retrieved manually by a Lara, Shull & May, LLC ("LSM") representative from the quarterly account statements provided by your custodian. The calculations for quarterly performance should be considered an approximation for planning purposes. For actual performance values please refer to account statements or documentation provided by the custodian. Performance percentages are calculated by dividing the difference between the current quarter's balance and the previous quarter's balance by the previous quarter's balance, and adjusting for any additions or withdraws in the quarter. These calculations do not meet AIMR and GAAP standards. Certain assets under LSM may not be shown, such as real estate, brokerage only, or private placement assets.

The end result

What you gain from completing the Retirement Success Solution®2 process will depend on your honest participation and commitment to your plan.

Most of the people I have worked with on this process tell me they feel more comfortable making the transition from employment to retirement after completing our Retirement Success Solution®2. They also enjoy the feeling of greater optimism that comes from working with an advisor who has a thorough understanding of their goals. Again, this is why having a knowledgeable planner in your corner to guide you is so vitally important.

Clients also tell me they like the fact that they have more effective tax and investment strategies in place after this process. They also appreciate how this system helps them clearly define and develop a set of achievable goals. Furthermore, clients feel more comfortable knowing their accountant and financial planner have conducted a "meeting of the minds" to find the best tax strategies available.

Why is all of this important? To me it's quite simple: I believe too many people are taking too much risk when it comes to saving for retirement. This is, in part, due to the lack of clearly defined and identified goals. Individuals too often have unrealistic expectations when it comes to returns, causing them to use investment vehicles that are more prone to wide fluctuations and losses. To combat this, the Retirement Success Solution®2, using the information you provide, will help outline your individual goals and determine the growth rate you need to achieve your retirement goals and to develop the strategies for achieving those goals.

Just do it!

CHAPTER NINE

Your Probability of Success

Now that you have completed the Retirement Funding Analysis, you should have a better idea of the dollar amount and growth rate needed in order to achieve your retirement goals.

Do these numbers seem overwhelming or unachievable? Or are you comfortable with your ability to reach these important milestones? Either way, you must keep in mind that your success, in part, will depend upon market forces that you (or I or anyone else) have zero control over. Welcome to the world of investing!

I don't want to paint a bleak picture though. When it comes to investing, I believe the key to success is identifying a realistic return based on financial market history and then identifying investment vehicles that will allow you to achieve whatever benchmark it is you have set.

In fact, looking at the history of the markets is a good place to start when trying to figure out what your probability of success will be. For example, from 1930 to 2009, I looked at how the Dow Jones Industrial Average (Dow) performed every 10 years and found there were only three times in this 80-year period that it provided a return of 10% or better. This occurred in the 1950's, 1980's and 1990's – all time periods which were marked by steep declines in interest rates.

In all the other 10-year periods when interest rates were either flat or on the rise, the Dow lost an average of 0.165% annually. That's right, minus 0.165% it is not a typo. That is no gain at all for those 50 years. Eliminating the depression years of the 1930's the average annual gain for the '40s, '60s, '70s and 2000 to 2009 was only 1.024%.

As I write this book in early 2011, the Federal Reserve continues to keep short-term rates near *zero. Am I mistaken, or is the only direction for interest rates to go UP???* If you combine this with the low value of the dollar compared to foreign currencies, surging oil and commodity prices, and larger budget deficits, the prospect for double digit returns over the next 10 years seems very unlikely.

On the brighter side, many corporations are flush with cash, corporate profits are increasing, productivity is improving and worldwide competition is keeping inflation in check – all of which are good things for you, me and other investors. In short, these factors will be positive for the equity markets. Nonetheless, double digit returns over the next 10 years shouldn't be expected, so you need to take this into account during your own planning.

The chart of the Dow Jones Industrial Average for the past 100 years (on the next page) shows a pretty spectacular gain. However, from the beginning of 1905, when the Dow stood at a low of 32.47, to the end of the year 2009, at its high of 10,428, the average annual growth rate is only 5.70%.

This period covers two World Wars, the Korean and Vietnam Wars, Desert Storm and the Iraq War, presidential assassinations, the Great Depression and many other events that spooked the market.

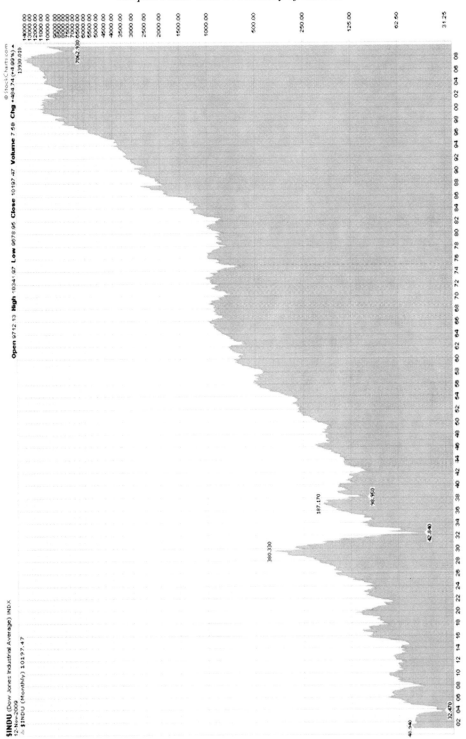

Clearly, you shouldn't base all of your investment decisions on the performance of the Dow stocks over a 100-year period. But given the size and importance of the Dow companies to the marketplace, they were picked as representatives of the overall market for a reason; it gives you an idea of how difficult it can be to achieve anything over a 10% annual return.

Actually, the probability of achieving even a 7% to 8% annual return is pretty low given market history. While these rates are certainly attainable, given the proper strategies and the right market conditions, there are still many factors, such as inflation and taxes, which can limit any returns your portfolio might create.

So where does this leave us? Well, I believe everyone needs to find a way to achieve their retirement goals using a much lower growth rate. If after completing the Retirement Funding Analysis you discovered your situation requires a 7% to 12% annual return on your investments, you might want to go back and begin to redefine and reprioritize your goals. Why? Because I can almost guarantee that it would take an extraordinary situation for you to see this type of growth rate consistently over a long period of time. Market history tells us this is the case even today.

Now, I am not saying the "sky is falling," but I am trying to paint an honest, realistic picture of what you should expect now and in the future. In fact, I believe we are currently entering a period of slowly rising interest rates over the next 10 – 15 years. And during this time, most analysts, including myself, foresee modest, single-digit growth in corporate earnings, which will be negated by the slow rise in interest rates.

What does this mean? Simply put, all of this can have a significant impact on what you can comfortably withdraw each year from your retirement savings; and because of this, we face the possibility of having to do more with less.

If you recall, achieving high growth rates in the 1980's and 1990's wasn't much of a problem, especially when the market witnessed an explosion of fast-moving, highly-touted tech stocks. Today's market looks more like it did in the 1960's and 1970's when growth rates averaged only 2% to 3%.

To further demonstrate my point, let's take a look at a chart prepared by Metropolitan Life Insurance Company which shows the probability of an individual's retirement assets lasting for 20, 25 and 30 years based on different withdrawal rates AND different stock/bond investment mixes.

20-Year Retirement
Stock/Bond Investment Mix

Withdrawal Rate	100/0	80/20	60/40	40/60	15/85	5/95
4%	96	98	99	99	99	99
5%	90	92	95	97	99	98
6%	78	81	**82**	81	69	48
7%	64	63	**57**	44	12	1

As you can see in the table above, with a 5% annual withdrawal rate, there is a strong probability, more than 90% across the realm of possible stock/bond investment mixes, of your retirement assets lasting 20 years. However, if the withdrawal rate needed is 6% per year, then you will need a 60/40 stock/bond mixture of investments in order to reach the highest probability of success: 82%. The lower the probability of success implies a greater possibility of depleting your assets. In this case, there's an 18% chance of running out of money within 20 years.

What happens if you need income at a 7% withdrawal rate each year? Well, this is where things get serious because the probability of achieving this withdrawal rate, even with an ideal 60/40 investment mix is only **57%** which implies a 43% probability of depleting your assets. Given this, you can see why it is very important to try to achieve your retirement objectives with a withdrawal rate of 5% or less.

But how does this change when looking at a 25 or 30-year retirement timeframe? Again, two charts produced by Metropolitan Life Insurance Company offer a look at what your probability of success will be for targeted withdrawal rates at different stock/bond investment mixes.

25-Year Retirement
Stock/Bond Investment Mix

Withdrawal Rate	100/0	80/20	60/40	40/60	15/85	5/95
4%	92	94	97	98	99	99
5%	81	83	83	80	69	42
6%	66	65	61	43	14	1
7%	48	43	33	12	0	0

30-Year Retirement
Stock/Bond Investment Mix

Withdrawal Rate	100/0	80/20	60/40	40/60	15/85	5/95
4%	87	88	89	90	86	71
5%	73	74	70	60	25	4
6%	56	53	42	25	1	0
7%	38	31	20	5	0	0

After reviewing the 25 and 30-year tables, you can see some definite differences, especially when you start looking at how your probability of success is lowered as your retirement timeframe is lengthened.

For example, close examination of the 20 and 25-year tables shows a big difference between the probabilities of your retirement assets lasting the entire time if your withdrawal rate is 6%. For a 20-year timeframe, you have an 82% probability of your assets lasting with a 60/40 mix of investments. But, this drops to 61%, using the same 60/40 investment mix, if the timeframe is increased to 25 years.

And if you really want a wake-up call, consider the figures shown in the 30-year table. Simply put, this chart alone strikes fear into the minds of individuals who thought their retirement assets would last forever.

Let's look at the probability of your retirement assets lasting 30 years. Using the same 60/40 investment mix, your probability of achieving a

6% annual withdrawal rate for the entire period is only 42% - as compared to 61% for 25 years and 82% for 20 years. How is this possible and what causes this to happen? Actually, it's pretty simple considering past history and well-documented market trends: over a 30-year period you are bound to experience a substantial bear market, and a bear market is further exacerbated when you are withdrawing assets from your investments.

Bottom line, given the present market situation and the future outlook, the odds of achieving any growth rate in excess of 6% (let alone 7%) over a period of time is highly unlikely. So, if this fits your situation, you need to start looking at how you will be taking your money out as well as how and when you will be spending your money.

And the time to do this is now; especially if you haven't retired yet. Planning ahead and re-adjusting your goals and investment strategies will leave you in a much better position. Better than waiting or doing nothing at all.

Everyone wants to be a success right? Well, when it comes to your retirement and being able to "succeed" at all those things you want to do and experience, it is no different than any other pursuit you might undertake you need to set goals, plan ahead and put some work into it in order to make it happen. Only then will your probability of success increase accordingly.

Due to the low probability of your retirement assets lasting greater than 30 years if you were withdrawing in excess of 5%, our Retirement Funding Analysis determines the growth rate that you must achieve in your pre-retirement years so that in your post retirement years you can achieve your goals with a 4% to 5% annual return.

It is OK to take some risk in your pre-retirement years because if you experience any market decline you can always postpone your retirement to allow more time to possibly recover assets that were lost, so that in retirement you only need to earn 4% to 5% annually.

I cannot over emphasize how important it is to do this analysis so that you can have the assets available to you in retirement to produce the income you desire with the least amount of risk.

You must determine your sustainable withdrawal rate, which is different from the growth rate needed to achieve your retirement income goals with an inflation factor.

What is a sustainable withdrawal rate?

A withdrawal rate is the percentage that is withdrawn each year from an investment portfolio. If you take $20,000 from a $1 million portfolio, your withdrawal rate that year is 2% ($20,000 divided by $1 million).

However, in retirement income planning, what's important is not just your withdrawal rate, but your sustainable withdrawal rate. A sustainable withdrawal rate represents the maximum percentage that can be withdrawn from an investment portfolio each year to provide income with the reasonable certainty that the income provided can be sustained as long as it's needed, throughout your lifetime.

Why is having a sustainable withdrawal rate important?

Your retirement lifestyle will depend not only on your assets and investment choices, but also on how quickly you draw down your retirement portfolio. Figuring out an appropriate withdrawal rate is a key factor in retirement planning. However, this presents many challenges and requires multifaceted analysis of many aspects of your retirement income plan. After all, it is getting more and more common for retirement to last 30 years or more, and a lot can happen during that time. Drawing too heavily from your investment portfolio, especially in the early years, could mean running out of money too soon. Take too little, and you might needlessly deny yourself the ability to enjoy your money. You want to find a rate of withdrawal that gives you the best chance to maximize income over your entire retirement period.

A sustainable withdrawal rate is critical to retirement planning, but it can apply to any investment portfolio that is managed with a defined timeframe in mind. It is also fundamental to certain types of mutual funds that are managed to provide regular payments over a specific time period. For example, some so-called distribution funds, which are often used to provide retirees with ongoing income, are designed to distribute all of an investor's assets by the time the fund reaches its targeted time horizon. As a result, the fund must calculate how much money can be distributed from the fund each year without exhausting its resources before that target date is reached.

Tip:

Each distribution fund has a unique way of addressing the question of what constitutes a sustainable withdrawal rate. Before purchasing this type of investment, be sure to obtain the prospectus from the fund and read it so you can carefully consider its investment objectives, risks, charges and expenses before investing.

How does a sustainable withdrawal rate work?

Perhaps the most well-known approach is to withdraw a specific percentage of your portfolio each year. In order to be sustainable, the percentage must be based on assumptions about the future, such as how long you will need your portfolio to last, your rate of return and other factors. It also must take inflation into account.

For example, John will have a $2,000,000 investment portfolio when he retires. He estimates that withdrawing $80,000 yearly, adjusted for inflation, will be adequate to meet his expenses. John's sustainable withdrawal rate is 4%, ($80,000 annual income divided by his investment portfolio of $2,000,000). John must make sure that his investment allocation is designed so that he can sustain this level of income without depleting his investments.

This is where Monte Carlo simulation comes into play. We have used our Retirement Funding Analysis to determine the growth rate you need to achieve your retirement income goals. We have also identified how much you need to withdraw from your investment portfolio each year.

Let's suppose you need $10,000 in monthly spendable income. In this example, our IRA Distribution and Income Tax Analysis determine that in order to net $10,000 each month, you will need $150,000 total gross income each year. The $150,000 accounts for an estimated $30,000 in federal and state income taxes so you can end up with $120,000 net income. This achieves your initial goal of $10,000 monthly spendable income.

Continuing to the next step using the above example, let's assume you have the following sources of annual retirement income:

Social Security Income:	$	24,000
Pension Income:	$	30,000
Total Income:	$	54,000

Total Annual Gross Income Desired:	$	150,000
Current Retirement Income:	$	(54,000)
Shortfall:	$	96,000

Thus, to achieve your $150,000 gross annual retirement income goal, you need additional income of $96,000.

Now assume you have $1,200,000 in investment assets.

The withdrawal amount divided by the value of your investment asset determines your annual withdrawal rate:

$96,000/$1,200,000 = 8.00\%$

Now, we need to know if 8.00% is a sustainable withdrawal rate. This is where Monte Carlo simulation comes into play.

By running a Monte Carol simulation on your investments as they are currently asset allocated we can determine the probability of your assets lasting your lifetime or for a certain number of years.

This is why having the proper asset allocation is so important. How do you know if you are properly asset allocated if you have not run a Monte Carlo simulation to determine the probability of achieving your goals?

Of course, inflation will play a big part in determining your withdrawal rate. This is where your financial advisor plays a key role. Your advisor should have the capability of doing a Monte Carlo analysis for you.

While Monte Carlo simulation is complex, let me try and explain how it works.

When you sit down with a financial professional to update your retirement plan, you are likely to encounter a Monte Carlo simulation; a financial forecasting method that has become popular in the last few years. Monte Carlo financial simulations project and illustrate the probability that you will reach your financial goals and can help you make better informed investment decisions.

Estimating investment returns

All financial forecasts must account for variables like inflation rates and investment returns. The catch is that these variables have to be estimated, and the estimate used is critical to forecast results. For example, a forecast that assumes stocks will earn an average of 4% each year for the next 20 years will differ significantly from a forecast that assumes an average annual return of 8% over the same time.

Estimating investment returns is particularly difficult. For instance, the volatility of stock returns makes short-term projections almost meaningless. Multiple factors influence investment returns, including events such as natural disasters and terrorist attacks, which are unpredictable. So, it's important to understand how different forecasting methods handle this inherent uncertainty.

Basic forecasting methods

Straight line forecasting methods assume a constant value for the projection. For example, a straight line forecast might show that a portfolio worth $116,000 today would have a future value of approximately $250,000 if the portfolio grows by an annual compounded return of 8% for the next 10 years. This projection is helpful, but it has a flaw. In the real world, returns aren't typically that consistent from year to year.

Forecasting methods that utilize "scenarios" provide a range of possible outcomes. Continuing with the 10 year example above, a "best case scenario" might assume that your portfolio will grow by an average 12% annual return and reach $360,000. The "most likely scenario" may assume an 8% return for a $250,000 value, and the "worst case scenario" might use 4%, resulting in a final value of roughly $171,000. Scenarios give you a better idea of the range of possible outcomes; however, they aren't very precise in estimating the likelihood of any specific result.

Forecasts that use Monte Carlo analysis are based on computer generated simulations. You may be familiar with simulations in other areas: for example, local weather forecasts are typically based on a computer analysis of national and regional weather data. Similarly, Monte Carlo financial simulations rely on computer models to replicate the behavior of economic variables, financial markets, and different investment asset classes.

Why is Monte Carlo simulation useful?

In contrast to more basic forecasting methods, Monte Carlo simulation explicitly accounts for volatility, especially the volatility of investment returns. It enables you to see the spectrum of thousands of possible outcomes, taking into account not only the many variables involved, but also the range of potential values for each of these variables.

By attempting to replicate the uncertainty of the real world, Monte Carlo simulation can actually provide a detailed illustration of how likely it is that a given investment strategy will meet your needs. When it comes to retirement planning, Monte Carlo simulation can help you answer specific questions such as:

- Given a certain set of assumptions, what is the probability that funds will run out before the age of 85?

- If that probability is unacceptably high, how much additional money would need to be invested each year to decrease the probability to 10%?

The mechanics of a Monte Carlo simulation

A Monte Carlo simulation typically involves hundreds of thousands of individual forecasts or "iterations," based on data that you provide (e.g. your portfolio, timeframes and financial goals). Each of these individual iterations draws a result based on the historical performance of every investment included in the simulation.

Each asset class, whether small-cap stocks, corporate bonds, large value stocks, etc., has an average (or mean) for a given period. Standard deviation measures the statistical variation of the actual return of that asset class around the average for that period. A higher standard deviation implies greater volatility. The returns for stocks have a higher standard deviation than the returns for U.S. Treasury Bonds, for instance.

There are different types of Monte Carlo computational methods, but each generates a forecast that reflects the variable patterns of investment returns. Software modeling stock returns, for example, might produce a series of annual returns such as the following: Year 1: -7%, Year 2: -9%, Year 3: +16%, and so on. For a 10 year projection, a Monte Carlo simulation will produce a series of 10 randomly generated returns, one for each year in the forecast, based on the model's inputs. A separate series of random returns is generated for each iteration in the simulation.

Example: Let's say a Monte Carlo simulation performs 1000 iterations using your current retirement assumptions and investment strategy. Of those 1000 iterations, 600 indicate that your assumptions will result in a successful outcome, while 400 iterations indicate that you will fall short of your goal. The simulation tells you that you have a 60% chance of successfully meeting your retirement goals.

An important note, especially for all the attorneys reading this: the projections or other information generated by Monte Carlo analysis tools regarding the likelihood of various investment outcomes are hypothetical in nature, do not reflect actual investment results and are not guarantees of future results. Results may vary with each use and over time.

Let us now look at a sample portfolio worth $1,000,000 consisting of the following asset classes with the specified percentages held in each asset class:

U.S. Stock	21.12%
International Stock	17.57%
Real Estate	1.94%
High Yield	8.05%
Fixed Income	33.28%
Absolute Return	17.04%
Cash	1.00%
	100.00%

In our first Monte Carlo simulation we will assume a 5% constant fixed withdrawal and see that the probability of the assets being worth more than $1,000,000 at the end of 25 years is 64%. When we ran the second example, the $1,000,000 portfolio with the same asset classes and the same percentage of holdings in each asset class but the 5% withdrawal increasing by 2% each year to take into account inflation, the probability of this portfolio being worth more than $1,000,000 at the end of 25 years was only 46.9%.

Wow, a greater than 50% chance your money will be less than what you start with. That is not encouraging. That is why it is so important to monitor your progress relative to your goal on a quarterly basis to make sure you are on track with your goals and make reductions in living expenses, if need be, to maintain your principal.

*****

Tips you can use

Here is a suggestion regarding mortgages that can help to reduce the growth rate, as well as the sustainable withdrawal rate, needed to achieve your retirement goal:

It might be a good idea to pay off your mortgage. Why? Even if you have been paying down your mortgage for over 15 years, the remaining balance will be quite high, see the table on the next page, and the total monthly payments divided by your remaining mortgage will be quite high.

For example, say your original mortgage was $300,000 at 6%. This means your monthly payment is around $1,798 or approximately $1,800 per month. After 15 years, your mortgage balance would still be $213,146. However, if we add up your payments for 12 months, we get approximately $21,600 ($1,800 x 12). This represents a 10.13 percent return on the $213,146 remaining balance if you pay it off early. Tell me, where are you going to get a 10.13% return with any degree of safety?

The following table, keeping with the assumption of an original 30-year mortgage of $300,000 at 6% and a monthly principal and interest payment of $1,798, illustrates this point and shows the remaining balance and the percentage return you would have to earn if you were to invest your remaining mortgage balance.

End of Year	Years Remaining		Remaining Balance	Total Annual Payments as % of remaining balance
1	29	$	296,315.96	7.28%
5	25	$	279,163.07	7.73%
10	20	$	251,057.17	8.60%
15	15	$	213,146.53	10.13%
16	14	$	204,105.57	10.57%
17	13	$	194,506.97	11.10%
18	12	$	184,316.36	11.71%
19	11	$	173,497.21	12.44%
20	10	$	162,010.76	13.32%
21	9	$	149,815.85	14.41%
22	8	$	136,868.78	15.77%
23	7	$	123,123.17	17.53%
24	6	$	108,529.76	19.89%
25	5	$	93,036.26	23.20%
26	4	$	76,587.16	28.18%
27	3	$	59,123.51	36.51%
28	2	$	40,582.73	53.18%
29	1	$	20,898.41	103.28%
30	0	$	-	0.00%

So, if you only have 10 years remaining on your mortgage, you should definitely pay it off as it would take a 13.32% return on the $162,010 to equal your monthly payments. However, if you decide against paying off your mortgage, please consider refinancing it as an interest only loan or a new 30-year mortgage to considerably lower your payment obligations.

Given all this, let me give you an idea of how the growth rate needed to achieve one's retirement income goals would be lowered if we paid off the above $162,010 remaining balance. Assuming we are looking for $75,000 of spendable income, have $20,000 in Social Security benefits, are 65 years old, have $900,000 in personal assets and are looking to live to age 92, the growth rate needed is 7.03%. However, if we pay off the mortgage and subtract the $162,010 from our $900,000 in personal assets, we now lower our retirement income needs from $75,000 annually to $53,400! This in turn lowers our growth rate to 5.36%. Needless to say, this is a significant outcome, as you would no longer have to take the risk of earning 7% (or more) per year. And because of this, you could then achieve all of your retirement goals by investing in U.S. government-guaranteed Ginnie Maes[1] – which, again, is another significant development.

Don't believe me? I encourage you to go to our website www.retirementsuccesssolution.com and complete the Retirement Funding Analysis (RFA) and input the numbers I just gave you (which include a 2% consideration/assumption for inflation and Social Security benefits).

CHAPTER TEN

Should You Do This
On Your Own?

One of the reasons our country is so great is that we, as citizens of the United States, have an amazing amount of freedom when it comes to how we make, manage and spend our money. Because of this, anyone preparing for retirement has a multitude of options when it comes to saving for it - stocks, bonds, IRAs, mutual funds, 401(k)s – to name but a few.

Furthermore, a society such as ours, overflowing with readily available information, makes it much easier to educate oneself on a wide variety of issues, including investing your money. Books, tapes, websites, magazines, and seminars are just a few examples of the sources out there for anyone interested in investing today. Some are good, some not so good, so a degree of caution is warranted as you tap into any of these resources, especially when employing the use of the Internet.

With all of these available resources, do I think people should undertake the monumental task of putting together and managing their own retirement portfolio? Unless you've had some type of professional training or education in investment strategies and/or tax planning, my answer is this: NO.

I believe the stakes are much too high for most individuals to go down the "retirement investment road" alone. Unfortunately, many people are not as knowledgeable about investing as they think they are - an observation based on my experiences with clients during my many years of providing financial planning counsel. In short, I can't tell you how many people, whom I have worked with, realize their previously self-managed portfolios weren't doing as well as they should have.

Given this, I believe it is much better for individuals to have a financial advisor who not only has a professional investment background, but also knows how to incorporate tax planning strategies into the equation. Tax planning know-how is very important because being able to match your tax strategies with your investment strategies is key to getting the most mileage (and value) out of your retirement savings.

Having said this, it is important to remember that an educated investor – one who understands the basics of the market and has a solid grasp of his/her financial goals – is a financial planner's best client. So even if you do seek out and employ the services of a professional advisor, don't quit the learning process on your end. When it's time to work with your advisor, the more intelligently you can discuss your retirement goals and needs, as well as the investment vehicles to be used, the more comfortable you will feel about the steps to be taken down-the-road.

Some of you might be asking, "Why should I pay someone to help manage my retirement money when I'll probably need every penny of it to do what I want to do?" Employing the services of an experienced financial advisor will cost you some money, but I can also tell you the investment guidance, implementation and expertise should put you in a much better position than doing it on your own. Additionally, a good advisor will help you stay-the-course and recommend sound adjustments to your portfolio based on market factors that could have a negative impact on your long-term savings.

With this in mind, I strongly recommend – if you haven't done so already – finding an experienced Certified Financial Planner (CFP®) to help you in the process of managing and investing your retirement assets. Why? Well, below is an excellent example of how "doing it on your own" can lead to disaster.

Recently, I was referred to an individual – we'll call him "Charlie" – who had been the chief financial officer of a large company. Charlie retired five years ago and felt he knew how to handle his investments. His attitude was: "No way am I going to pay a 1% asset management fee, and no way am I going to pay a CPA to give me professional tax advice or prepare my tax return." In addition, he didn't think it was important to pay an attorney to draft his Will, let alone provide him with the estate planning strategies which could save his children over $2,000,000 in future estate taxes. Bottom line, Charlie knew it all and didn't want any help.

By the time I met Charlie he was in the fifth year of his "I'll do it myself" approach. And after encountering some serious setbacks, he was now searching for someone who could coordinate all of his tax and investment planning. In short, he had learned a lesson – the hard way.

Some of the errors, in my opinion, he had made solely on his own. For example, he had made a lucrative real estate investment that carried a 12% interest rate secured by real estate assets. However, he made it personally so he had to pay the federal and state income taxes on the 12% interest. If he had made the investment with his IRA assets, rather than his personal assets, he could have sheltered the 12% interest from ordinary income taxes. Real estate in an IRA? Yes, you can make real estate investments in an IRA. And if you have the right type of IRA that allows for alternative investments, you can also invest in hard assets like gold and silver, real estate, promissory notes, and collectibles such as art, coins, and stamps. Keep in mind, I am not recommending these as investments, but if you are an expert in any of these areas you should be aware that these options are available and offer you a way to invest in a personal area of expertise – which is something Charlie would have known if he had consulted a financial planning professional from the start.

Charlie also had something I like to call "index sickness." He had invested most of his assets in the S&P index, which, unfortunately, is made-up mostly of large cap stocks, some of which have not done well over the past five years. Furthermore, he hadn't properly asset allocated his assets to achieve the growth rate he needed. Given this, it also came as no surprise that Charlie didn't even know the growth rate he needed to earn to achieve his retirement goals.

Here is a brief overview of the damage Charlie had done to his own portfolio. He had withdrawn 5% of his assets from an index fund.

Unfortunately, he started in January of 2000 and had not properly asset allocated his assets. Charlie's assets which originally totaled $1,000,000 had declined to $318,492 by September 30, 2009! So he lost over 68% of his retirement assets and the probability of achieving his retirement goals is now highly unlikely.

Look at the chart below:

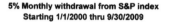

5% Monthly withdrawal from S&P index
Starting 1/1/2000 thru 9/30/2009

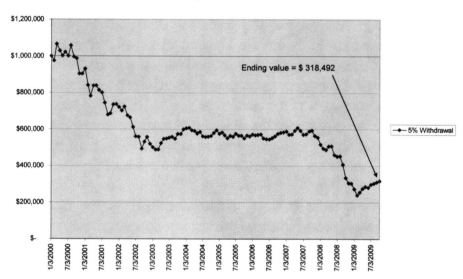

If Charlie had asset allocated his assets between the five asset classes outlined below, the final value of his account would have been $1,034,989 by September 30, 2009, even if he had withdrawn 5% annually. The lesson in all of this is simple: there is a big difference between losing over 62% of your retirement nest egg and having more than you originally invested at the end of 10 years.

	Initial Investment	Ending Value
S&P 500 - Large Cap Growth	$ 200,000	$ 72,924
Russell - Mid Cap Value	$ 200,000	$ 289,262
Dow Jones Real Estate	$ 200,000	$ 346,831
Lehman Brothers Intermediate Gov.'t	$ 200,000	$ 221,953
Russell Top 200 Value	$ 200,000	$ 104,019
Total Investment	**$ 1,000,000**	**$ 1,034,989**

The above are Exchange Traded Funds, ETFs, and are representative of funds in their asset classes. One of the asset classes shown above lost over 50% of its value and another, the Russell Top 200 Value, lost approximately 50% of its value; however, the other classes did well, even with the 5% withdrawal. The point is, if Charlie had asset allocated, he would have done extremely well – even in a negative market. This, my friends, is the whole point (and advantage) of asset allocation. Keep in mind there is no guarantee that the above asset classes will perform as they did in this example. Investing involves an element of risk but asset allocation can reduce that risk and volatility.

*****

Tips you can use

If you plan on trying to "go it alone," you need to – at a minimum – subscribe to a research service like Morningstar. By doing so, you can research the various fund managers and rank them by performance in their respective asset classes. Keep in mind, though, you should not just look at past performance. Why? Well, if the manager is a top manager in his/her asset class the general trend is they may be best positioned to do well when that particular asset class does well.

Case in point: in December 1999, a former client of mine came to me complaining about the horrible performance of his real estate mutual funds and the poor performance of his mid-cap value managers. He wanted a greater percentage of his portfolio in high tech stocks, which were soaring in late 1999. We had been rebalancing his account, that is selling his high tech stocks and reinvesting in real estate and value oriented stocks which had under performed in late 1999. He didn't believe in rebalancing and pulled his account and went into large cap growth stocks – primarily tech-related stocks – on his own. Yes, real estate did poorly in 1998 and 1999, but REIT funds averaged over 20% a year from January 2000 to December 2004. Value stocks, which did poorly in 1998 and 1999, did extremely well over the next five years. Given this, it doesn't take much to guess what has probably happened to this person's money, at least what is left of it.

Now, of course, real estate has done poorly over the last two years, but that is the point of asset allocation – you do not know which asset class will do well, so it is important to be diversified by asset class. I know this advice sounds like a song coming from a broken record, but if this is the only thing you get out of this book, I will be happy. And so will you, in the long run.

CHAPTER ELEVEN

What to Look For
in a Financial Advisor

My wife is always reminding me, "You get what you pay for." And this certainly holds true when it comes to finding the right financial advisor to help you with the important task of managing your retirement funds.

Keep in mind, this doesn't mean the most expensive advisor will give you the best advice and get you the best returns. What's more important is finding an advisor who shares your investment philosophy and operates on the same wavelength that you do. In short, your advisor needs to be someone you can connect with and respect. This alone will go a long way toward building a trusting and beneficial relationship, one that can help you reach your retirement goals.

How do you find someone like this? Well, many of my clients are referred to me by their own friends, family and/or business acquaintances – all of whom have had good experiences with our firm and the services we offer. Given this, I'd recommend that you ask your own friends and family for names of professional financial advisors they might know. If they can't point you in the right direction, there are some easily accessible resources you can tap into for current information on credible, experienced advisors in your area. There is a wealth of information available to consumers regarding the firms and/or individuals they use to help them with investments and retirement planning.

One great place to start is the Financial Planning Association (FPA) in Denver, Colorado. As a professional association, they offer a referral service and can also provide great background information on the industry as a whole. Any reputable financial planner or advisor is going to belong to this group. You can find them at www.fpanet.org.

Another good place to look for background information is the Financial Industry Regulatory Authority (FINRA) at www.FINRA.org. This is an important resource because this is where you can review a broker or broker/dealer's history, as well as find out if any disciplinary actions have been taken against them.

Prior actions against a professional should always be taken into consideration before using their services. If, in fact, you do discover some type of action has been taken against them, make sure you ask them about this – it is something the person should be able to address and explain with complete honesty. A person with multiple violations should probably be avoided, and, by all means, stay away from anyone who has been disciplined for "unauthorized transactions."

I also believe it is important to hire a financial planner who utilizes asset allocation software as a part of their services. If they have this, they should be able to tell you how much to invest in each asset class in order to achieve your desired growth rate with the least amount of risk. In addition, a good financial advisor should also be able to provide you information about themselves and their practice, as well as offer you reports on the managers of all the funds they invest in on behalf of their clients.

You will be doing yourself a big favor by conducting your own due diligence and thoroughly checking out a financial planner before engaging them to help you with your retirement portfolio. Remember to ask the planner questions, ask for references and check-up on them with the tools you have available via the Internet and professional associations.

A good example of why asking questions and checking references is so important is illustrated by an individual I met several years ago who had approximately $700,000 to invest. During our meeting, he told me how he had been presented with a proposal from a so-called financial planner who recommended that he invest in the Kingdom Fund which GUARANTEED a 2% return PER MONTH. (Folks, the only guarantees I am counting on in life are death and taxes.)

Needless to say, this individual had not been presented with a copy of the advisor's ADV Part II Brochure (more on that later); didn't see a SIPC plaque in the office; and thought it all sounded too good to be true. To his credit, he furnished me with the information and I passed it on to the Securities and Exchange Commission (SEC) office in Philadelphia. Several months later the SEC brought enforcement action against several individuals involved in what was a ponzi scheme – one that targeted religious based investors under the guise of being a fellow religious financial planner. Any reluctance to share other information (like credentials, references, etc.) should be a red flag.

Bottom line, it's ultimately up to you – the investor – to be the biggest, most vocal, protector of your money. Why? Well, it's YOUR money and it's YOUR livelihood and retirement at stake. Given this, you should do whatever you can in your power to safeguard these hard-earned dollars. If it means educating yourself about investing – then do it. If it means asking lots of questions and demanding satisfactory answers – then do it. If it means interviewing more than one financial planner until you find someone you like and feel comfortable with – then do it. Why? Because if you don't, no one else will!

Also, please note that a financial advisor must have passed the Uniform Investment Adviser Law Examination series 65 or 66 and be registered with an investment advisor (firm) and applicable states in order to provide investment advisory services and receive fees. There is a difference between a financial advisor charging an asset management fee and an individual that is able to buy or sell securities for a commission. Some individuals are dually registered so they can wear both hats, so to speak.

In order to buy or sell securities and receive commissions, an individual must be an active broker agent registered with a broker/dealer and have passed FINRA's series 6 or 7 and the 63 or 66 exam. For more information regarding the types of securities each exam enables an individual to engage in, please visit www.finra.org.

*****

Tips you can use

Whether you are starting a new account or transferring existing accounts, here are a few questions you should ask any Certified Financial Planner before putting your money in their care:

Question: **How will you determine what investments are best for me and my situation?**
Comments: They should tell you a retirement funding analysis of your needs will be done to determine the growth rate needed to achieve your goals. They should discuss with you your financials and investment risk tolerance. Once this is completed, your funds should be asset allocated to target your goals and fall in line with your suitability requirements.

Question: **What are you fees?**
Comments: Remember, you get what you pay for, so getting financial planning advice (and related services) for free is not necessarily a good goal. Paying 1% to 1.5% of assets under management is an average fee, but if you want to implement a "buy and hold" strategy than a brokerage account, commission based, may be more cost effective than a fee based account. Some advisors use C Share mutual funds in which you do not pay a fee, but the planner receives anywhere from .80% to 1.00% from the mutual fund as a 12(b)-1 fee. This is usually more economical if the planner is recommending several mutual funds, along with individual bonds; this way, you are not paying a fee for the planner to hold the bonds. Keep in mind, because of the C share trail, if you end up holding C shares longer than three years, you could end up paying more in the long run than you would if you had purchased the A share class that incurred an upfront sales charge. So, it is important that you be realistic about, and discuss your holding time period with your advisor.

Question: **Can I have a copy of your Form ADV Part II Brochure?**
Comments: You should DEFINITELY receive this before you leave their office. An investment advisor firm is required to provide this to you at the onset of the relationship or upon your request. In addition, you

should also be given a Supplement disclosure about the advisor providing advice and/or of any advisor which has discretionary authority over your account. In short, it will explain a lot about their practice and list any disciplinary action taken against them from a regulatory agency, such as the FINRA, SEC or any state government securities and/or insurance commissioners.

Question: **Can I have the names and numbers of one or two of your clients for a reference call?**
Comments: A planner should jump at the chance to provide you with the names of his clients. They will likely refer you to only good clients, but you can learn a lot about your future financial planner by speaking to these clients – especially if you were not referred to this planner from an existing client.

Question: **Who will hold my securities?**
Comments: Remember the Bernie Madoff scandal? Bernie's firm held his clients assets and prepared all the customers statements, making it easy to forge statements. If you are dealing with a small firm owned by an individual and they are holding the securities, make sure you can see what securities you own and all the transactions that are being made. Most planners have a third party broker/dealer relationship and custody arrangements to hold clients' assets, with the large brokerage firms, such as Merrill Lynch, RBC Capital Markets or Morgan Stanley, usually holding their own. Some individuals prefer to have these "name" firms hold their assets because they are familiar with them. But for the most personalized, hands-on professional service, I recommend looking for a Certified Financial Planner in a smaller, independent firm. FINRA, the SEC and the Dodd-Frank Act have created numerous industry changes regarding custody regulations. To find out more, go to www.sec.gov and search for Dodd-Frank Act.

Question: **Can I see your SIPC plaque?**
Comments: By having this on display, it simply means their broker/dealer is a member of the Securities Investor Protection

Corporation (SIPC). This doesn't protect your account against losses, but it does provide protection if the brokerage firm holding your securities goes under. Also check that the CUSTODIAN of your account is a member of SIPC. For more information, go to www.sipc.org.

Question: **How often will I get statements for my accounts?**
Comments: At minimum, you should receive quarterly account statements, but the information should be available to you anytime upon request. The statements should be sent directly from the custodian of your accounts.

Question: **What happens if my account declines in value?**
Comments: Your account will likely go down (or lose value) some quarters, so you must be prepared for this. However, your declines can be minimized and your long-term progress smoother if your funds are properly asset allocated. Given this, the planner should explain the process of rebalancing your portfolio (especially in a declining market), which should be done at least annually. Do not switch advisors just because your account declines in value. If you are properly asset allocated, your account should not decline as much as the averages. In addition, if you have top quartile managers, your account should recover quickly as the market rebounds.

Question: **I have heard of an Investment Policy Statement (IPS). What exactly is an IPS?**
Comments: An Investment Policy Statement or IPS offers guidelines for: 1) determining the growth rate you need to achieve; 2) establishing the timeframe needed to achieve your goals; and 3) detailing your investment plan's asset allocation. If you do not receive an IPS, how do you know what the advisor's objectives are?

Question: **What fees will I have to pay if I decide to pull my accounts?**
Comments: You should have very few fees to pay if you decide to change planners. Most likely, you will pay a prorated quarterly fee, or a

few commissions to sell securities if you want to transfer cash. There may be a fee charged by your custodian for closing your account. Refer to your custodial agreement regarding fees charged, if any. However, if you are changing firms, I recommend you transfer your assets-in-kind. This will eliminate the temptation for your present (pre-change) planner/broker to charge you a high commission for selling your securities. Also, your new planner will charge you few, if any commissions to liquidate your previous holdings to re-asset allocate those assets into his/her recommendations.

Question: **How important is honesty and integrity to you?**

Comments: While most individuals in the financial planning service industry uphold a high degree of honesty and integrity, there are a few who will take advantage of your ignorance. Don't hesitate to contact the FINRA if you suspect dishonesty (of any type) has taken place. However, I would first contact the planner's supervisor (if there is one) before you contact the FINRA, as a more immediate response to your complaint(s) would likely come from them.

CHAPTER TWELVE

Investment Product Overview

As I have already outlined in earlier chapters, there are a number of different ways you can invest your retirement savings. However, it is important to keep in mind that how you asset allocate your retirement portfolio to achieve the growth rate needed to successfully realize your retirement income objectives is critical to your overall success.

I say this because not all investment opportunities offer the returns and/or performance over the long-term you will need in order to meet your retirement goals. Given this, it is important you educate yourself on what certain investment vehicles can, and cannot do. Doing this will better prepare you for conversations with your financial advisor, as well as help you better determine what kinds of investments you're most comfortable with in terms of risks and possible returns.

Or think of it this way: Your investments will be some of the biggest purchases made during your lifetime. For example, before buying a home, you find out as much as you can about the house you are interested in, and you might even visit it a few times before making a decision. The same goes for buying a car – you do your research, test drive it, and even ask others what they think about it. My point is this: You need to take the same care and do the same research and fact-finding when deciding where to invest money in your retirement portfolio.

Keeping all this in mind, here are a number of investment options and strategies you might want to consider for your retirement portfolio:

1) As discussed earlier, an asset allocated portfolio consists of different asset classes. This can easily be achieved by using mutual funds which are managed for a specific asset class. For instance, if you need a portion of your portfolio to be in international stocks, it is much easier to invest in a mutual fund whose primary objective is international growth, as opposed to investing in individual international companies. You could select a private manager to do this for you if your portfolio is over $1,000,000, but you can also select an excellent international mutual fund on your own if you do your homework.

2) Consider using the services of a Certified Financial Planner who uses an asset allocation software program. There are several reputable companies that offer this service. Your portfolio could include 10 – 15 top managers who are constantly supervising and rebalancing in response to market fluctuations.

3) If the growth rate needed to achieve your retirement objective is less than 5%, you will probably have a portion of it in fixed income investments. If this is the case, consider Ginnie Mae, Fannie Mae and/or Freddie Mac mortgage-backed bonds[1] to provide you with a monthly interest check. Currently, today in mid-2011, these mortgage-backed bonds are yielding between 4.0% and 4.5% (or higher), are rated AAA and Ginnie Mae's are backed by the full faith and credit of the U.S Government. Before 2008, I recommended some AAA mortgage-backed securities from very reputable mortgage companies such as Countrywide Mortgage and Washington Mutual (WAMU). Little did I know that this country was going to have the severe mortgage crisis we are now experiencing. Fortunately, most of the mortgage-backed bonds we recommended were Ginnie Mae, Fannie Mae or Freddie Mac[1].

4) If you need to have a portion of your assets in short-term maturity assets there are short-term U.S. Treasury Bonds!

Despite their obvious advantages, I rarely meet a new client who has invested in them. One-year Treasury Notes currently yield less than 1% and are exempt from state income taxes. Thus, a 1% Treasury yield is equivalent to 1.2% for a resident in a state with a 6 % state income tax. For a slightly higher yield, your advisor should be able to offer you competitive certificates of deposits from a number of banks.

Another consideration for your fixed income portfolio is in international bonds which can act as a hedge against a falling dollar on international markets. With our current record deficits the future outlook for interest rates and the U.S. dollar is gloomy. I expect interest rates to rise over the next two to five years and for the U.S. dollar to decline as our deficits increase. Thus, I recommend a portion of your retirement assets be invested in International bonds as a hedge against a declining dollar.

5) With the prospect of rising commodity prices – due to the demand from markets in China, India and other developing nations – a natural resource or commodity fund may be a consideration in a portfolio where the growth rate needed is in excess of 6%.

6) While I'm not a big fan of variable annuities[3], they have changed over the past few years. The most important feature of a variable annuity is its option to provide lifetime income to the annuity holder no matter what happens to the underlying assets. If you're married, there are lifetime income options to purchase for you and your spouse. This way you have the peace of mind in knowing that your income will not run out. However, if you're planning on leaving your retirement assets to your children you should think twice about purchasing a variable annuity. The expense ratio on variable annuities is usually in excess of 3%; that along with a 5% withdrawal, results in an 8% withdrawal from your investment account. There have been very few times

(since 1950 in 25 year incremental periods) when an 8% withdrawal still left assets in the investment account.

7) Once you have selected several mutual fund managers to invest with, preferably with the guidance of a Certified Financial Planner, you can check their performance relative to other asset managers in their respective class. Hopefully, they will all be top quartile managers. There is really no reason why you should place your investments in the care of anyone but the best, right?

8) Stick with quality. Philip Carret, who founded the Pioneer Fund in 1927, gave me some advice which I have never forgotten. He said, "More people lose more money going after a little more yield than for any other reason." Stick with quality bonds. I steer away from BBB bonds or lower and favor AAA mortgage-backed bonds from Freddie Mac, Fannie Mae or better still Ginnie Mae[1].

9) Make sure your investment advisor gives you an Investment Policy Statement (IPS) that clearly lays out the objectives you are trying to achieve, the time horizon, the asset allocation and, most importantly, the growth rate you are trying to achieve.

10) Another consideration is using a tactical Exchange-Traded Funds asset manager who will have your assets diversified among several asset classes using Exchange-Traded Funds (ETFs) for those asset classes. The manager has the ability to diversify your assets amongst the various asset classes based on their analysis of current market conditions. Tactical asset managers did extremely well in the Fall of 2008 when the market declined approximately 40%. In mid-August one group we know of repositioned their clients primarily in government and corporate bonds, and more importantly, in cash - avoiding the steep decline. They also can have a much lower expense ratio than regular mutual funds. Another advantage of using ETFs is that they are very tax efficient. ETFs are structured for tax efficiency and can be more

attractive than mutual funds. While ETFs can sell securities and the gain or loss is passed through, their turnover is much less than a traditional mutual fund. In the U.S., whenever a mutual fund realizes a capital gain that is not balanced by a realized loss, the mutual fund must distribute the capital gains to its shareholders. This can happen whenever the mutual fund sells portfolio securities, whether to reallocate its investments or to fund shareholder redemptions. These gains are taxable to all shareholders, even those who reinvest the capital gains distributions in more shares of the fund. In contrast, ETFs are not redeemed by holders (instead, holders simply sell their ETF shares on the stock market, as they would a stock). Investors generally only realize capital gains when they sell their own shares or when the ETF trades to reflect changes in the underlying index.

While most financial advisors are honest, be aware of the too good to be true. A good example is Alan Stanford. He had offices in all the major cities and sold Certificates of Deposits to investors. The red flag was his yields were always the highest. In the end, Stanford's investors lost more than a billion dollars because they wanted that extra 1% or 2% yield. Bernie Madoff's clients turned a blind eye to his consistently superior returns when all other managers were having their ups and downs. Deal only with reputable firms and check your broker's credentials and a review of any disciplinary action by going to www.FINRA.com and conducting a Broker Check.

CHAPTER THIRTEEN

Conclusion:
Making it All Work
For You

As I have tried to demonstrate throughout this book, there are many important things to consider when investing for retirement. The key is to find a way to separate the good information from the bad, and use this knowledge to your advantage. Hopefully, it will boost your retirement portfolio.

If you look around today, you can see we are bombarded by all kinds of information regarding investment opportunities. Magazines tell us about "hot stocks", print ads tout "great investment opportunities", and a plethora of websites provide instant access to all sorts of real-time information about where we should put our money. Even cable television offers programs with "experts" giving anyone watching a firsthand look at what's happening in the markets on a minute-by-minute basis. Put all these together, with the hundreds of investment-related books on the market today, and you can see how it can become a confusing mix to sort through.

I will be the first to tell you there are plenty of dangers out there when it comes to finding good places to invest your money. But, I can personally say that I cannot think of one person that has lost money in the market after using a well-diversified portfolio for 10 years or more. This is possible because they have successfully separated marketing messages from reality and found a way to effectively distribute their hard-earned dollars amongst a host of credible, well-established investment opportunities (most often with the help of an experienced and reputable advisor).

For this reason, I cannot reiterate too often how important asset allocation is to the long-term health (and growth) of your retirement portfolio. Bottom line, this is one of your most important keys to success, but it is a process that must be regularly monitored in order to maximize your returns over the long run. In addition to evaluating your managers each year, you should also review your accounts to rebalance your portfolio to its original percentage allocation.

Here is how rebalancing works: certain asset classes will have appreciated in value while some may have decreased in value, over the past year. The managers that have appreciated in value now have a greater percentage of your portfolio assets. By selling assets from the appreciated managers and reinvesting in the managers that have declined, you will restore your portfolio to its original asset allocation balance – the one that is designed to achieve the growth rate needed to realize your retirement goals. Rebalancing has been shown to add between 1.5% and 2.0% annually to a portfolio's overall gross performance.

Fortunately, I have found that many people understand the importance of asset allocation in order to avoid the danger of "putting all their eggs (money) in one basket." However, despite the asset allocating many people employ, I have yet to meet anyone who has rebalanced their portfolio on their own. In fact, this is a step most people avoid altogether and will only do after we have reviewed its importance.

So, when it comes to figuring out your best course of action for asset allocation and/or rebalancing your portfolio, enlist the help of a qualified and trusted financial advisor. Even I – an experienced financial planner – tap into the knowledge of other professionals to manage my money. In fact, I currently have a leading asset allocation financial service firm managing a good portion of my own retirement portfolio because they manage money through a long time approach of asset allocation. If this is something I do, doesn't it make sense you should consider it as well?

Bottom line, you owe it to yourself to do something – and to do it now. Why? Because waiting to take the important steps I have outlined in this book can cost you money – money you could be using to achieve your retirement goals and dreams.

Do not hesitate to contact me with any questions you might have or suggestions for my next book on having a successful retirement. My business e-mail is ronl@larashullmay.com. I welcome all your comments and questions.

So start now, and by all means, enjoy your retirement!

RESOURCES

Listed below are websites that can provide some useful information:

www.retirementsuccesssolution.com – This website has several online tools you will find useful. The primary online tool is the Retirement Funding Analysis which determines the growth rate you need to achieve your retirement income goal. In addition, we have a minimum distribution calculator, education funding analysis and other tools you will find of interest.

www.finance.yahoo.com – This is a great website to track all of your security holdings if your current investment firm does not provide you with internet access to your accounts.

www.closedendfund.com – The Closed End Fund Association website is an excellent place to find information on various closed-end funds. This website also lists discount to net assets values, allows you to search funds by category or yield and much, much more.

www.fpanet.org – The Financial Planning Association (FPA) website is a good location to search for a Certified Financial Planner (CFP®).

www.finra.org – The Financial Industry Regulatory Authority (FINRA) regulates all the stock brokers. This is a great site to find any disciplinary history on your advisor or broker.

https://Us.pioneerinvestments.com – Pioneer Funds website is a wonderful website to compare Uni-K, SEP IRA, Profit Sharing and Simple IRA plans to see which is most advantageous for your situation.

www.cboe.com – The Chicago Board of Exchange (CBOE) gives information on options. They offer several online tutorials for you to learn about options and how they can help protect and enhance your portfolio.

www.retirementliving.com – This website has tons of information on places to live during retirement and many tax saving ideas.

DISCLOSURES

[1] *Mortgage-backed Securities: Ginnie Mae, Fannie Mae & Freddie Mac*

Ginnie Mae is the common name for Government National Mortgage Association. Ginnie Mae's are guaranteed by the full faith and credit of the U.S. Government. That does not mean you can get your investment back at any time. It means the principal will eventually be paid back based on principal payments being met on an amortized amount. One of the risks of Ginnie Mae's is interest rate risk. If you invest in a 5% Ginnie Mae at par (100) and next year interest rates have increased to 6% for new Ginnie Mae's and you wish to sell your 5% Ginnie Mae it will be worth less than par or 100.

The other risk of Ginnie Mae's is prepayment risk. For example if you purchase a 6% Ginnie Mae at par or 100 and are counting on getting that 6% income for several years and interest rates decline due to the amount of refinances and sales of home resulting in mortgages being paid off prematurely, this will result in you receiving your principal back earlier than you thought. This can be a problem because now you have to reinvest your principal, but at a lower interest rate. To protect from this considering investing in lower coupon Ginnie Mae selling at a discount. Thus, if principal is paid back earlier than expected, it will be paid back at par resulting in a higher yield to maturity than you originally invested. Find out more about Ginnie Mae's by visiting their website at: http://www.ginniemae.gov/index.asp

[2] *The Retirement Success Solution® (RSS)*

The RSS is a planning process intended to identify your personal and lifestyle goals and develop strategies to help best achieve them. Investment plans created in response to these goals are not guaranteed, are subject to market and investment risk, potential for principal loss and no assurance of appreciation is made.

³ *Variable Annuity*

What is a Variable Annuity?

A variable annuity is a contract between you and an insurance company, under which the insurer (insurance company) agrees to make periodic payments to you, beginning either immediately or at some future date. You purchase a variable annuity contract by making either a single purchase payment or a series of purchase payments.

A variable annuity offers a range of investment options. The value of your investment as a variable annuity owner will vary depending on the performance of the investment options you choose. The investment options for a variable annuity are typically mutual funds that invest in stocks, bonds, money market instruments or some combinations of the three.

Although variable annuities are typically invested in mutual funds, variable annuities differ from mutual funds in several important ways:

First, variable annuities let you receive **periodic payments** for the rest of your life (or the life of your spouse or any other person you designate). This feature offers protection against the possibility that after you retire you will outlive your assets.

Second, variable annuities have a **death benefit**. If you die before the insurer has started making payments to you, your beneficiary is guaranteed to receive a specified amount – typically at least the amount of your purchase payments. Your beneficiary will get a benefit from this feature if, at the time of your death, your account value is less than the guaranteed amount.

Third, variable annuities are **tax-deferred**. That means you pay no taxes on the income and investment gains from your annuity until you withdraw your money. You may also transfer your money from one investment option to another within a variable annuity without paying tax at the time of the transfer. When you take your money out of a variable annuity, however, you will be taxed on the earnings at ordinary income tax rates rather than lower capital gains rates. In general, the benefits of tax deferral will outweigh the costs of a variable annuity only if you hold it as a long-term investment to meet retirement and other long-range goals.

> **Caution!**
> Other investment vehicles such as IRAs and employer-sponsored 401(k) plans may also provide you with tax-deferred growth and other tax advantages. For most investors, it will be advantageous to make the maximum allowable contributions to IRAs and 401(k) plans before investing in a variable annuity.
> In addition, if you are investing in a variable annuity through a tax-advantaged retirement plan (such as a 401(k) plan or IRA), you will get **no additional tax advantage** from the variable annuity. Under these circumstances, consider buying a variable annuity only if it makes sense because of the variable annuity's other features, such as lifetime income payments and death benefit protection. The tax rules that apply to variable annuities can be complicated – before investing, you may want to consult a tax advisor about the tax consequences to you from investing in a variable annuity.

Remember: Variable annuities are designed to be long-term investments to meet retirement and other long-range goals. Variable annuities are not suitable for meeting short-term goals because substantial taxes and insurance company charges may apply if you withdraw your money early. Variable annuities also involve investment risks, just as mutual funds do.

How Variable Annuities Work

A variable annuity has two phases: an **accumulation phase** and a **payout phase.**

During the **accumulation phase,** you make purchase payments which you can allocate to a number of investment options. For example, you could designate 40% of your purchase payments to a bond fund, 40% to a U.S. stock fund and 20% to an international stock fund. The money you have allocated to each mutual fund investment option will increase or decrease over time, depending on the fund's performance. In addition, variable annuities often allow you to allocate part of your purchase payments to a fixed account. A fixed account, unlike a mutual fund, pays a fixed rate of interest. The insurance company may reset this interest rate periodically, but it will usually provide a guaranteed minimum (i.e. 3% per year).

Example: You purchase a variable annuity with an initial purchase payment of $10,000. You allocate 50% of that purchase payment ($5,000) to a bond fund and 50% ($5,000) to a stock fund. Over the following year, the stock fund has a 10% return and the bond fund has a 5% return. At the end of the year, your account has a value of $10,750 ($5,500 in the stock fund and $5,250 in the bond fund), minus fees and charges (discussed below).

Your most important source of information about a variable annuity's investment options is the prospectus. Request the prospectuses for the mutual fund investment options. Read them carefully before you allocate your purchase payments among the investment options offered. You should consider a variety of factors with respect to each fund option, including the fund's investment objectives and policies, management fees and other expenses that the fund charges, the risks and volatility of the fund, and whether the fund contributes to the diversification of your overall investment portfolio. The SEC's online publication, *Mutual Fund Investing: Look at More Than a Fund's Past Performance*, provides information about these factors. Another SEC online publication, *Invest Wisely: An Introduction to Mutual Funds*, provides general information about the types of mutual funds and the expenses they charge.

During the accumulation phase, you can typically transfer your money from one investment option to another without paying tax on your investment income and gains, although you may be charged by the insurance company for transfers. However, if you withdraw money from your account during the early years of the accumulation phase, you may have to pay "surrender charges," which are discussed below. In addition, you may have to pay a 10% federal tax penalty if you withdraw money before the age of 59½.

At the beginning of the **payout phase**, you may receive your purchase payments plus investment income and gains (if any) as a lump-sum payment, or you may choose to receive them as a stream of payments at regular intervals (generally monthly).

If you choose to receive a stream of payments, you may have a number of choices of how long the payments will last. Under most annuity contracts, you can choose to have your annuity payments last for a period that you set (such as 20 years) or for an indefinite period (such as your lifetime or the lifetime of you and your spouse or other beneficiary). During the payout phase, your annuity contract may permit you to choose between receiving payments that are fixed in amount or payments that vary based on the performance of mutual fund investment options.

The amount of each periodic payment will depend, in part, on the time period that you select for receiving payments. Be aware that some annuities do not allow you to withdraw money from your account once you have started receiving regular annuity payments.

In addition, some annuity contracts are structured as **immediate annuities**, which means that there is no accumulation phase and you will start receiving annuity payments right after you purchase the annuity.

The Death Benefit and Other Features

A common feature of variable annuities is the **death benefit**. If you die a person you select as a beneficiary (such as your spouse or child) will receive the greater of: (i) all the money in your account, or (ii) some guaranteed minimum (such as all purchase payments minus prior withdrawals).

Example: You own a variable annuity that offers a death benefit equal to the greater of: account value or total purchase payments minus withdrawals. You have made purchase payments totaling $50,000. In addition, you have withdrawn $5,000 from your account. Because of these withdrawals and investment losses, your account value is currently $40,000. If you die, your designated beneficiary will receive $45,000 (the $50,000 in purchase payments you put in minus $5,000 in withdrawals).

Some variable annuities allow you to choose a 'stepped-up" death benefit. Under this feature, your guaranteed minimum death benefit may be based on a greater amount than purchase payments minus withdrawals. For example, the guaranteed minimum might be your account value as of a specified date, which may be greater than purchase payments minus withdrawals if the underlying investment options have performed well. The purpose of a stepped-up death benefit is to "lock in" your investment performance and prevent a later decline in the value of your account from eroding the amount that you expect to leave to your heirs. This feature carries a charge however, which will reduce your account value.

Variable annuities sometimes offer other optional features, which also have extra charges. One common feature, the guaranteed minimum income benefit, guarantees a particular minimum level of annuity payments, even if you do not have enough money in your account (perhaps because of investment losses) to support that level of payments. Other features may include long-term care insurance, which pays for home health care or nursing home care if you become seriously ill.

You may want to consider the financial strength of the insurance company that sponsors any variable annuity you are considering buying. This can affect the company's ability to pay any benefits that are greater than the value of your account in mutual fund investment options, such as a death benefit, guaranteed minimum income benefit, long-term care benefit, or amounts you have allocated to a fixed account investment option.

Caution!
You will pay for each benefit provided by your variable annuity. Be sure you understand the charges. Carefully consider whether you need the benefit. If you do need the benefit, consider whether you can buy the benefit more cheaply as part of the variable annuity or separately (*e.g.,* through a long-term care insurance policy).

Variable Annuity Charges

You will pay several charges when you invest in a variable annuity. Be sure you understand all the charges before you invest. **These charges will reduce the values of your account and the return on your investment.** Often they will include the following:

- **Surrender charges** – If you withdraw money from a variable annuity within a certain period after a purchase payment (typically within six to eight years, but sometimes as long as 10 years), the insurance company usually will assess a "surrender" charge, which is a type of sales charge. This charge is used to pay your financial professional a commission for selling the variable annuity to you. Generally the surrender charge is a percentage of the amount withdrawn, and declines gradually over a period of several years, known as the "**surrender period**." For example, a 7% charge might apply in the first year after a purchase payment, 6% in the second year, 5% in the third year, and so on until the eighth year, when the surrender charge no longer applies. Often contracts will allow you to withdraw part of your account value each year – 10% or 15% of your account value, for example – without paying a surrender charge.

  Example: You purchase a variable annuity contract with a $10,000 purchase payment. The contract has a schedule of surrender charges, beginning with a 7% charge in the first year, and declining by 1% each year. In addition, you are allowed to withdraw 10% of your contract value each year free of surrender charges. In the first year, you decide to withdraw $5,000, or one-half of your contract value of $10,000 (assuming that your contract value has not increased or decreased because of investment performance). In this case, you could withdraw $1,000 (10% of contract value) free of surrender charges, but you would pay a surrender charge of 7%, or $280, on the other $4,000 withdrawn.

- **Mortality and expense risk charge** – This charge is equal to a certain percentage of your account value, typically in the range of 1.25% per year. This charge compensates the insurance company for insurance risks it assumes under the annuity contract. Profit from the mortality and expense risk charge is sometimes used to pay the insurer's costs for selling the variable annuity, such as a commission paid to your financial professional for selling the variable annuity to you.

  Example: Your variable annuity has a mortality and expense risk charge at an annual rate of 1.25% of account value. Your average account value during the year is $20,000, so you will pay $250 in mortality and expense risk charges that year.

- **Administrative fees** – The insurer may deduct charges to cover record-keeping and other administrative expenses. This may be charged as a flat account maintenance fee (perhaps $25 or $30 per year) or as a percentage of your account value (typically in the range of 0.15% per year).

  Example: Your variable annuity charges administrative fees at an annual rate of 0.15% of account value. Your average account value during the year is $50,000. You will pay $75 in administrative fees.

- **Underlying Fund Expenses** – You will also indirectly pay fees and expenses imposed by the mutual funds that are the underlying investment options for your variable annuity.

- **Fees and Charges for Other Features** – Special features offered by some variable annuities such as a **stepped-up death benefit**, a **guaranteed minimum income benefit**, or **long-term care insurance**, often carry additional fees and charges.

Other charges, such as initial sales loads, or fees for transferring part of your account from one investment option to another, may also apply. You should ask your financial professional to explain to you all charges that may apply. You can also find a description of the charges in the prospectus for any variable annuity that you are considering.

Tax-Free "1035" Exchanges

Section 1035 of the U.S. tax code allows you to exchange an existing variable annuity contract for a new annuity contract without paying any tax on the income and investment gains in your current variable annuity account. These tax-free exchanges, known as 1035 exchanges, can be useful if another annuity has features that you prefer, such as a larger death benefit, different annuity payout options, or a wider selection of investment choices.

You may, however, be required to pay surrender charges on the old annuity if you are still in the surrender charge period. In addition, a new surrender charge period generally begins when you exchange into the new annuity. This means that for a significant number of years (as many as 10 years), you typically will have to pay a surrender charge (which can be as high as 9% of your purchase payments) if you withdraw funds from the new annuity. Further, the new annuity may have higher annual fees and charges than the old annuity, which will reduce your returns.

> **Caution!**
> If you are thinking about a 1035 exchange, you should compare both annuities carefully. Unless you plan to hold the new annuity for a significant amount of time, you may be better off keeping the old annuity because the new annuity typically will impose a new surrender charge period. Also, if you decided to do a 1035 exchange, you should talk to your financial professional or tax advisor to make sure the exchange will be tax-free. If you surrender the old annuity for cash and then buy a new annuity, you will have to pay tax on the surrender.

Bonus Credits

Some insurance companies are now offering variable annuity contracts with "bonus credit" features. These contracts promise to add a bonus to your contract value based on a specified percentage (typically ranging from 1% to 5%) of purchase payments.

Example: You purchase a variable annuity contract that offers a bonus credit of 3% on each purchase payment. You make a purchase payment of $20,000. The insurance company issuing the contract adds a bonus of $600 to your account.

> **Caution!**
> Variable annuities with bonus credits may carry a downside, however – higher expenses that can outweigh the benefit of the bonus credit offered.

Frequently, insurers will charge you for bonus credits in one or more of the following ways:

- **Higher surrender charges** – Surrender charges may be higher for a variable annuity that pays you a bonus credit than for a similar contract with no bonus credit.

- **Longer surrender periods** – Your purchase payments may be subject to surrender charges for a longer period than they would be under a similar contract with no bonus contract.

- **Higher mortality and expense risk charges and other charges** – Higher annual mortality and expense risk charges may be deducted for a variable annuity that pays you a bonus credit. Although the difference may seems small, over time it can add up. In addition, some contracts may impose a separate fee specifically to pay for the bonus credit.

Before purchasing a variable annuity with a bonus credit, ask yourself –

and the financial professional who is trying to sell you the contract – whether the bonus is worth more to you than any increased charges you will pay for the bonus. This may depend on a variety of factors, including the amount of the bonus credit and the increased charges, how long you hold your annuity contract, and the return on the underlying investments. You also need to consider the other features of the annuity to determine whether it is a good investment for you.

Example: You make purchase payments of $10,000 in Annuity A and $10,000 in Annuity B. Annuity A offers a bonus credit of 4% on your purchase payment, and deducts annual charges totaling 1.75%. Annuity B has no bonus credit and deducts annual charges totaling 1.25%. Let's assume that both annuities have an annual rate of return, prior to expenses, of 10%. By the tenth year, your account value in Annuity A will have grown to $22,978. But, your account value in Annuity B will have grown more, to $23,136, because Annuity B deducts lower annual charges, even though it does not offer a bonus.

You should also note that a bonus may only apply to your initial purchase payment, or to purchase payments you make within the first year of the annuity contract. Further, under some annuity contracts the insurer will take back all bonus payments made to you within the prior year or some other specified period if you make a withdrawal, if a death benefit is paid to your beneficiaries upon your death, or in other circumstances.

Caution!

If you already own a variable annuity and are thinking of exchanging it for a different annuity with a bonus feature, you should be careful. Even if the surrender period on your current annuity contract has expired, a new surrender period generally will begin when you exchange that contract for a new one. This means that, by exchanging your contract, you will forfeit your ability to withdraw money from your account without incurring substantial surrender charges. And as described above, the schedule of surrender charges and other fees may be higher on the variable annuity with the bonus credit than they were on the annuity that you exchanged.

Example: You currently hold a variable annuity with an account value of $20,000, which is no longer subject to surrender charges. You exchange that annuity for a new variable annuity, which pays a 4% bonus credit and has a surrender charge period of eight years, with surrender charges beginning at 9% of purchase payments in the first year. Your account value in this new variable annuity is now $20,800.

During the first year you hold the new annuity, you decide to withdraw all of your account value because of an emergency situation. Assuming that your account value has not increased or decreased because of investment performance, you will receive $20,800 minus 9% of your $20,000 purchase payment, or $19,000. This is $1,000 less than you would have received if you had stayed in the original variable annuity, where you were no longer subject to surrender charges.

In short: Take a hard look at bonus credits. In some cases, the "bonus" may not be in your best interest.

Ask Questions Before You Invest

Financial professionals who sell variable annuities have a duty to advise you as to whether the product they are trying to sell is suitable to your particular investment needs. Don't be afraid to ask them questions and write down their answers, so there won't be any confusion later as to what was said.

Variable annuity contracts typically have a "free look" period of 10 or more days, during which you can terminate the contract without paying any surrender charges and get back your purchase payments (which may be adjusted to reflect charges and the performance of your investment). You can continue to ask questions in this period to make sure you understand your variable annuity before the "free look" period ends.

Before you decide to buy a variable annuity, consider the following questions:

- Will you use the variable annuity primarily to save for retirement or a similar long-term goal?

- Are you investing in the variable annuity through a retirement plan or IRA (which would mean that you are not receiving any additional tax-deferral benefit from the variable annuity)?

- Are you willing to take the risk that your account value may decrease if the underlying mutual fund investment options perform badly?

- Do you understand the features of the variable annuity?

- Do you understand all of the fees and expenses that the variable annuity charges?

- Do you intend to remain in the variable annuity long enough to avoid paying any surrender charges if you have to withdraw money?

- If a variable annuity offers a bonus credit, will the bonus outweigh any higher fees and charges that the product may charge?

- Are there features of the variable annuity, such as long-term care insurance, that you could purchase more cheaply separately?

- Have you consulted with a tax advisor and considered all the tax consequences of purchasing an annuity, including the effect of annuity payments on your tax status in retirement?

- If you are exchanging one annuity for another, do the benefits of the exchange outweigh the costs, such as any surrender charges you will have to pay if you withdraw your money before the end of the surrender charge period of the new annuity?

Remember: Before purchasing a variable annuity, you owe it to yourself to learn as much as possible about how they work, the benefits they provide, and the charges you will pay.

[4] *Mutual Funds*

Before investing in mutual funds, it is important that you understand the sales charges, expenses, and management fees that you will be charged, as well as the breakpoint discounts to which you may be entitled. Understanding these charges and breakpoint discounts will assist you in identifying the best investment for your particular needs and may help you reduce the cost of your investment. This disclosure will give you general background information about these charges and discount. However, sales charges, expenses, management fees and breakpoint discounts vary from mutual fund to mutual fund. Therefore, you should discuss these issues with your Financial Advisor and review each mutual fund's prospectus and statement of additional information, which are available from your Financial Advisor, to get the specific information regarding the charges and breakpoint discounts associated with a particular mutual fund.

Sales Charges

Investors that purchase mutual funds must make certain choices, including which funds to purchase and which share class is most advantageous. Each mutual fund has a specified investment strategy. You need to consider whether the mutual fund's investment strategy is compatible with your investment objectives. Additionally, most mutual funds offer different share classes. Although each share class represents a similar interest in the mutual fund's portfolio, the mutual fund will charge you different fees and expenses depending upon your choice of share class. As a general rule, Class A shares carry a "front-end" sales charge or "load" that is deducted from your investment at the time you buy fund shares. This sales charge is a percentage of your total purchase. As explained below, many mutual funds offer volume discounts to the front-end sales charge assessed on Class A shares at certain pre-determined levels of investments; called "breakpoint discounts." In contrast, Class B and C shares usually do not carry any front-end sales charges. Instead, investors that purchase Class B or C shares pay asset-based annual service fees, which may be higher than those charges associated with Class A shares. Investors that purchase Class B and C shares may also be required to pay a sales charge, known as a contingent deferred sales charge ("CDSC"), when the they sell their shares, depending upon the rules of the particular mutual fund. In some instances, the CDSC may equal the front-end sales charge applicable to A shares. Generally, B shares are more inexpensive for investors with an intermediate to long-term time horizon and less than $100,000 to invest. C shares can be more expensive for investors over the long-term. In order to compare the expenses associated with each type of share class, please review the FINRA's Expense Analyzer available at:

http://apps.finra.org/investor_Information/ea/1/mfetf.aspx

Some fund companies also make their funds available through other share classes with different fee structures, including funds without sales charges, or no-load funds. In addition, some funds may be available through fee-based programs or accounts. Clients do not pay sales charges in these accounts; instead they offer mutual funds via an asset based annual fee.

Breakpoint Discounts

Most mutual funds offer investors a variety of ways to qualify for breakpoint discounts on the sales charge associated with the purchase of Class A shares. In general, most mutual funds provide breakpoint discounts to investors who make large purchases at one time. The extent of the discount depends upon the size of the purchase. Generally, as the amount of the purchase increases, the percentage used to determine the sales load decreases. In fact, the entire sales charge may be waived for investors that make very large purchases of Class A shares. Mutual fund prospectuses contain tables that illustrate the available breakpoint discounts and the investment levels at which breakpoint discounts apply. Additionally, most mutual funds allow investors to qualify for breakpoint discounts based upon current holdings from prior purchases through *"Rights of Accumulation,"* and future purchases based upon *"Letters of Intent."* This document provides general information regarding *Rights of Accumulation* and *Letters of Intent.*

However, mutual funds have different rules regarding the availability of *Rights of Accumulation* and *Letters of Intent.* Therefore, you should discuss these issues with your Financial Advisor and review the mutual fund prospectus to determine the specific terms upon which a mutual fund offers *Rights of Accumulation* or *Letters of Intent.*

Rights of Accumulation

Many mutual funds allow investors to count the value of previous purchases of the same fund, or another fund within the same fund family, with the value of the current purchase to qualify for the breakpoint discounts. Moreover, mutual funds allow investors to count existing holdings in multiple accounts, such as IRAs or accounts at other broker-dealers, to qualify for breakpoint discounts. Therefore, if you have accounts at other broker-dealers and wish to take advantage of the balances in these accounts to qualify for a breakpoint discount, you must advise your Financial Advisor about those balances. You may need to provide documentation to your Financial Advisor, establishing the holdings in those other accounts, if you wish to rely upon balances in accounts at another firm. In addition, many mutual funds allow investors to count the value of holdings in accounts of certain related parties, such as spouses or children, to qualify for breakpoint discounts. Each mutual fund has different rules that govern when relatives may rely upon each other's holdings to qualify for breakpoint discounts. You should consult with your Financial Advisor or review the mutual fund's prospectus or statement for additional information to determine what the rules are for the fund family in which you are investing. If you wish to rely upon the holdings of related parties to qualify for a breakpoint discount, you should advise your Financial Advisor about these accounts. You may need to provide your Financial Advisor with documentation if you wish to rely upon balances in accounts at another firm. Mutual funds also follow different rules to determine the value of existing holdings. Some funds use the current net asset value (NAV) of existing investments in determining whether an investor qualifies for a breakpoint discount. However, a small number of funds use the historical cost, which is the cost of the initial purchase, to determine the eligibility for breakpoint discounts. If the mutual fund uses historical cost, you may need to provide account records, such as confirmation statements or monthly statements, to qualify for a breakpoint discount based upon previous purchases. You should consult with your Financial Advisor and review the mutual fund's prospectus to determine whether the mutual fund uses either NAV or historical costs to determine breakpoint eligibility.

Letters of Intent

Most mutual funds allow investors to qualify for breakpoint discounts by signing a Letter of Intent, which commits the investor to purchasing a specified amount of Class A shares within a defined period of time, usually 13 months. For example, if an investor plans to purchase $50,000 worth of Class A shares over a period of 13 months, but each individual purchase would not qualify for a breakpoint discount, the investor could sign a Letter of Intent at the time of the first purchase and receive the breakpoint discount associated with a $50,000 investment on the first and all subsequent purchases. Additionally, some funds offer retroactive Letters of Intent that allow investors to rely upon purchases in the recent past to qualify for a breakpoint discount. However, if an investor fails to invest the amount required by the Letter of Intent, the fund is entitled to retroactively deduct the correct sales charges based upon the amount that the investor actually invested. If you intend to make several purchases within a 13-month period, you should consult your Financial Advisor and the mutual fund prospectus to determine if it would be beneficial for you to sign a Letter of Intent. As you can see, understanding the availability of breakpoint discounts is important because it may allow you to purchase Class A shares at a lower price. The availability of breakpoint discounts may save you money and may also affect your decision regarding the appropriate share class in which to invest. Therefore, you should discuss the availability of breakpoint discounts with your Financial Advisor and carefully review the mutual fund prospectus and its statement of additional information, which you can get from your Financial Advisor, when choosing among the share classes offered by a mutual fund. If you wish to learn more about mutual fund share classes or breakpoints, review the investor alerts on the FINRA website at:

http://www.finra.org/investorinformation/investoralerts/

or visit the many mutual fund websites available to the public.

[5] *Life Settlement*

What is a life settlement?

In a "life settlement" transaction, a life insurance policy owner sells his or her policy to an investor in exchange for a lump sum payment. The amount of the payment from the investor to the policy owner is generally less than the death benefit on the policy, but more than its cash surrender value. The dollar amount offered by the investor usually takes into account the insured's life expectancy (age and health) and then the terms and conditions of the insurance policy.

Why would a policy owner wish to sell a life insurance policy?

Due to changed family or other circumstances, a life insurance policy owner may no longer need the insurance provided by the policy. A spouse may have died, children may have grown up, or a company with life insurance on a key officer may have been sold or gone out of business. Other policy owners may have difficulty making premium payments or simply need cash. In such circumstances, many policy owners surrender their policies or let their policies lapse by ceasing to make premium payments. Selling a policy to an investor may be another alternative. Such sales may be made through life settlement brokers who charge commissions.

How does a life settlement take place and who are the parties involved?

A policy owner may discuss a possible settlement with his or her insurance agent or financial advisor, who then contacts a life settlement broker. In some cases, the policy owner may be solicited directly by a life settlement broker. Life settlement brokers may also be life insurance agents or securities brokers. Depending on the requirements of the states in which they do business, life settlement brokers may be licensed.

The life settlement broker obtains the insured's authorization to release medical records and forwards the policy owner's application and medical information to one or more companies known as life settlement providers. Many states, but not all, regulate life settlement providers, who also charge a commission.

The life settlement provider obtains life expectancy estimates on the insured and bids on the application. Life expectancy underwriters (who are not the insured's personal physician) evaluate the risk of mortality of the insured based on his or her personal characteristics. If the life settlement provider's bid is accepted, the provider may add that policy to a large group of policies, interests in which may be offered to investors. Institutional investors analyze the information provided by the life settlement provider, often obtaining their own life expectancy estimates. Retail investors, on the other hand, may have to rely on life settlement personnel or other investment professionals to assess the advantages and disadvantages of the transaction. In either case, the investor makes a cash payment to the policy owner or policy owners and continues to pay premiums necessary to keep the policy or policies in effect. Upon the insured's death, the investor receives the death benefit.

Considerations for Investors in Life Settlements

Before investing in a life settlement, investors may wish to keep the following points in mind:

- The return on life settlement depends on the insured's life expectancy and the date of the insured's death. As a result, the accuracy of a life expectancy estimate is essential. If the insured dies before his or her estimated life expectancy, the investor may receive a higher return. If the insured lives longer than expected, the investor's return will be lower. If the insured lives long enough or if the life expectancy is miscalculated, additional premiums may need to be paid and the cost of the investment could be greater than anticipated.

- Under certain circumstances, the investor may not receive the death benefit. For example, the life insurance company that issued the policy may refuse to pay out the death benefit if it believes the policy was sold under fraudulent circumstances. In addition, the heirs of the insured may challenge the life settlement or the insurance company may go out of business.

- The competence of a life expectancy underwriter and the accuracy of the life expectancy estimate are critical to the return on a life settlement. For the most part, life expectancy underwriters are not licensed or registered by state insurance regulators, and information about the methodologies and review procedures that life expectancy underwriters use is not generally disclosed.

- Life settlements can give rise to privacy issues. Insured individuals generally wish to keep their medical records and personal information confidential. Investors, on the other hand, want access to the insured's medical and other personal information to assess the advisability of their investment and to monitor it on a continuing basis.

Get More Information from the Regulators

Investors may want to determine whether professionals involved in a life settlement transaction are registered or licensed. To check on the licensing or registration status of a life settlement broker or provider, contact your state insurance regulator. Contact information is available on the website of the National Association of Insurance Commissioners (www.naic.org). To check on the registration status of a securities broker, use the Financial Industry Regulatory Authority's on-line BrokerCheck (www.finra.org).

More information can be obtained at:

http://www.sec.gov/investor/alerts/lifesettlements-bulletin.htm

Appendices

<u>Appendix 1</u>

Additional expenses I will need to cover in retirement:

	Amount needed:	$
_____	Amount needed:	$ _____
_____	Amount needed:	$ _____
_____	Amount needed:	$ _____
_____	Amount needed:	$ _____
_____	Amount needed:	$ _____
_____	Amount needed:	$ _____
_____	Amount needed:	$ _____
_____	Amount needed:	$ _____
_____	Amount needed:	$ _____
_____	Amount needed:	$ _____

Total needed: $ _____

Appendix 2

States with No State Income Tax*

1) Alaska

2) Florida

3) Nevada

4) South Dakota

5) Texas

6) Washington

7) Washington

8) Wyoming

New Hampshire and Tennessee limit their state income taxes to only dividends and interest income.

*As of 7/2011

Appendix 3

Single Life Mortality Table

Exact	Male			Female		
age	Death	Number of	Life	Death	Number of	Life
	probability a	lives b	expectancy	probability a	lives b	expectancy
50	0.57%	92,041	28.8	0.33%	95,460	32.5
51	0.62%	91,520	27.9	0.35%	95,147	31.6
52	0.67%	90,955	27.1	0.38%	94,811	30.7
53	0.71%	90,350	26.3	0.41%	94,450	29.8
54	0.75%	89,710	25.5	0.43%	94,067	28.9
55	0.79%	89,037	24.7	0.46%	93,659	28.1
56	0.85%	88,331	23.9	0.50%	93,224	27.2
57	0.91%	87,584	23.1	0.54%	92,759	26.3
58	0.98%	86,790	22.3	0.59%	92,256	25.5
59	1.06%	85,940	21.5	0.65%	91,708	24.6
60	1.16%	85,026	20.7	0.72%	91,109	23.8
61	1.26%	84,039	19.9	0.80%	90,452	23.0
62	1.37%	82,978	19.2	0.87%	89,732	22.1
63	1.48%	81,843	18.5	0.94%	88,951	21.3
64	1.59%	80,635	17.7	1.02%	88,113	20.5
65	1.72%	79,354	17.0	1.10%	87,217	19.7
66	1.86%	77,992	16.3	1.20%	86,257	18.9
67	2.02%	76,540	15.6	1.31%	85,223	18.2
68	2.20%	74,993	14.9	1.44%	84,105	17.4
69	2.40%	73,344	14.2	1.59%	82,891	16.6
70	2.62%	71,586	13.6	1.76%	81,571	15.9
71	2.87%	69,710	12.9	1.95%	80,132	15.2
72	3.15%	67,707	12.3	2.15%	78,566	14.5
73	3.44%	65,578	11.7	2.36%	76,875	13.8
74	3.76%	63,323	11.1	2.57%	75,064	13.1

Exact age	Male			Female		
	Death probability a	Number of lives b	Life expectancy	Death probability a	Number of lives b	Life expectancy
75	4.13%	60,942	10.5	2.82%	73,134	12.4
76	4.54%	58,427	9.9	3.12%	71,068	11.8
77	4.99%	55,774	9.3	3.44%	68,852	11.1
78	5.48%	52,990	8.8	3.79%	66,483	10.5
79	6.02%	50,086	8.3	4.18%	63,963	9.9
80	6.63%	47,073	7.8	4.63%	61,289	9.3
81	7.32%	43,954	7.3	5.16%	58,449	8.8
82	8.07%	40,737	6.8	5.75%	55,433	8.2
83	8.89%	37,449	6.4	6.41%	52,246	7.7
84	9.79%	34,119	6.0	7.16%	48,895	7.2
85	10.80%	30,778	5.6	8.00%	45,395	6.7
86	11.92%	27,456	5.2	8.94%	41,764	6.2
87	13.17%	24,183	4.8	10.00%	38,029	5.8
88	14.57%	20,998	4.5	11.18%	34,226	5.4
89	16.10%	17,939	4.1	12.47%	30,400	5.0
90	17.76%	15,051	3.8	13.89%	26,608	4.6
91	19.56%	12,378	3.6	15.43%	22,911	4.3
92	21.48%	9,957	3.3	17.10%	19,375	4.0
93	23.52%	7,818	3.1	18.88%	16,062	3.7
94	25.66%	5,979	2.9	20.77%	13,030	3.4
95	27.79%	4,445	2.7	22.69%	10,324	3.2
96	29.87%	3,209	2.5	24.60%	7,982	3.0
97	31.86%	2,251	2.4	26.47%	6,018	2.8
98	33.72%	1,534	2.2	28.28%	4,425	2.7
99	35.40%	1,017	2.1	29.97%	3,174	2.5
100	37.17%	657	2.0	31.77%	2,223	2.4

Appendix 4

Two lives, male and female, joint and survivor, female is the younger age (continued)

Female	Male	Exp.	Female	Male	Exp.	Female	Male	Exp.
59	92	28.4	60	102	27.4	62	64	29.2
59	93	28.4	60	103	27.4	62	65	28.9
59	94	28.4	60	104	27.4	62	66	28.6
59	95	28.4	60	105	27.4	62	67	28.3
59	96	28.4	60	106	27.4	62	68	28
59	97	28.4	60	107	27.4	62	69	27.8
59	98	28.4	60	108	27.4	62	70	27.6
59	99	28.4	60	109	27.4	62	71	27.4
59	100	28.4	60	110	27.4	62	72	27.2
59	101	28.4	61	61	30.9	62	73	27
59	102	28.3	61	62	30.5	62	74	26.9
59	103	28.3	61	63	30.1	62	75	26.7
59	104	28.3	61	64	29.8	62	76	26.6
59	105	28.3	61	65	29.5	62	77	26.5
59	106	28.3	61	66	29.2	62	78	26.4
59	107	28.3	61	67	28.9	62	79	26.3
59	108	28.3	61	68	28.7	62	80	26.2
59	109	28.3	61	69	28.5	62	81	26.2
59	110	28.3	61	70	28.3	62	82	26.1
60	60	31.8	61	71	28.1	62	83	26.1
60	61	31.4	61	72	27.9	62	84	26
60	62	31.1	61	73	27.8	62	85	26
60	63	30.7	61	74	27.6	62	86	25.9
60	64	30.4	61	75	27.5	62	87	25.9
60	65	30.1	61	76	27.4	62	88	25.9
60	66	29.9	61	77	27.3	62	89	25.8
60	67	29.6	61	78	27.2	62	90	25.8
60	68	29.4	61	79	27.1	62	91	25.8
60	69	29.2	61	80	27.1	62	92	25.8
60	70	29	61	81	27	62	93	25.8
60	71	28.9	61	82	27	62	94	25.7
60	72	28.7	61	83	26.9	62	95	25.7
60	73	28.6	61	84	26.9	62	96	25.7
60	74	28.4	61	85	26.8	62	97	25.7
60	75	28.3	61	86	26.8	62	98	25.7
60	76	28.2	61	87	26.8	62	99	25.7
60	77	28.1	61	88	26.7	62	100	25.7
60	78	28.1	61	89	26.7	62	101	25.7
60	79	28	61	90	26.7	62	102	25.7
60	80	27.9	61	91	26.7	62	103	25.7
60	81	27.9	61	92	26.7	62	104	25.7
60	82	27.8	61	93	26.6	62	105	25.7
60	83	27.8	61	94	26.6	62	106	25.7
60	84	27.7	61	95	26.6	62	107	25.6
60	85	27.7	61	96	26.6	62	108	25.6
60	86	27.7	61	97	26.6	62	109	25.6
60	87	27.6	61	98	26.6	62	110	25.6
60	88	27.6	61	99	26.6	63	63	29
60	89	27.6	61	100	26.6	63	64	28.6
60	90	27.6	61	101	26.6	63	65	28.3
60	91	27.5	61	102	26.6	63	66	27.9
60	92	27.5	61	103	26.6	63	67	27.6
60	93	27.5	61	104	26.5	63	68	27.3
60	94	27.5	61	105	26.5	63	69	27.1
60	95	27.5	61	106	26.5	63	70	26.9
60	96	27.5	61	107	26.5	63	71	26.6
60	97	27.5	61	108	26.5	63	72	26.4
60	98	27.5	61	109	26.5	63	73	26.3
60	99	27.5	61	110	26.5	63	74	26.1
60	100	27.5	62	62	29.9	63	75	26
60	101	27.5	62	63	29.5	63	76	25.8

Two lives, male and female, joint and survivor, female is the younger age (continued)

Female	Male	Exp.	Female	Male	Exp.	Female	Male	Exp.
63	77	25.7	64	91	24.1	65	106	23
63	78	25.6	64	92	24	65	107	23
63	79	25.5	64	93	24	65	108	23
63	80	25.4	64	94	24	65	109	23
63	81	25.3	64	95	24	65	110	23
63	82	25.3	64	96	24	66	66	26.2
63	83	25.2	64	97	24	66	67	25.8
63	84	25.2	64	98	24	66	68	25.5
63	85	25.1	64	99	23.9	66	69	25.2
63	86	25.1	64	100	23.9	66	70	24.9
63	87	25	64	101	23.9	66	71	24.6
63	88	25	64	102	23.9	66	72	24.4
63	89	25	64	103	23.9	66	73	24.1
63	90	24.9	64	104	23.9	66	74	23.9
63	91	24.9	64	105	23.9	66	75	23.8
63	92	24.9	64	106	23.9	66	76	23.6
63	93	24.9	64	107	23.9	66	77	23.4
63	94	24.9	64	108	23.9	66	78	23.3
63	95	24.9	64	109	23.9	66	79	23.2
63	96	24.8	64	110	23.9	66	80	23
63	97	24.8	65	65	27.1	66	81	22.9
63	98	24.8	65	66	26.8	66	82	22.9
63	99	24.8	65	67	26.4	66	83	22.8
63	100	24.8	65	68	26.1	66	84	22.7
63	101	24.8	65	69	25.8	66	85	22.6
63	102	24.8	65	70	25.5	66	86	22.6
63	103	24.8	65	71	25.3	66	87	22.5
63	104	24.8	65	72	25	66	88	22.5
63	105	24.8	65	73	24.8	66	89	22.4
63	106	24.8	65	74	24.6	66	90	22.4
63	107	24.8	65	75	24.5	66	91	22.4
63	108	24.8	65	76	24.3	66	92	22.4
63	109	24.8	65	77	24.2	66	93	22.3
63	110	24.8	65	78	24	66	94	22.3
64	64	28	65	79	23.9	66	95	22.3
64	65	27.7	65	80	23.8	66	96	22.3
64	66	27.3	65	81	23.7	66	97	22.3
64	67	27	65	82	23.6	66	98	22.2
64	68	26.7	65	83	23.6	66	99	22.2
64	69	26.4	65	84	23.5	66	100	22.2
64	70	26.2	65	85	23.5	66	101	22.2
64	71	25.9	65	86	23.4	66	102	22.2
64	72	25.7	65	87	23.4	66	103	22.2
64	73	25.5	65	88	23.3	66	104	22.2
64	74	25.4	65	89	23.3	66	105	22.2
64	75	25.2	65	90	23.2	66	106	22.2
64	76	25.1	65	91	23.2	66	107	22.2
64	77	24.9	65	92	23.2	66	108	22.2
64	78	24.8	65	93	23.2	66	109	22.2
64	79	24.7	65	94	23.2	66	110	22.2
64	80	24.6	65	95	23.1	67	67	25.3
64	81	24.5	65	96	23.1	67	68	24.9
64	82	24.5	65	97	23.1	67	69	24.6
64	83	24.4	65	98	23.1	67	70	24.3
64	84	24.3	65	99	23.1	67	71	24
64	85	24.3	65	100	23.1	67	72	23.7
64	86	24.2	65	101	23.1	67	73	23.5
64	87	24.2	65	102	23.1	67	74	23.3
64	88	24.2	65	103	23	67	75	23.1
64	89	24.1	65	104	23	67	76	22.9
64	90	24.1	65	105	23	67	77	22.7

Ron Lara is available for speaking engagements and personal appearances. For more information contact Ron at:

Virginia Office
Lara, Shull & May, LLC
7600 Leesburg Pike, Suite 120E
Falls Church, VA 22043
Phone: 703-827-2300
Toll Free: 800-842-8834

Colorado Office
Lara, Shull & May, LLC
610 E. Main Street
PO Box 2744
Frisco, CO 80443
Phone: 970-668-5700
Toll Free: 877-543-5444

Email: ronl@larashullmay.com

To order additional copies of this book or to see a complete list of all *Advantage Books*™ titles, visit our online bookstore at:

www.advbookstore.com
or
call our toll free number at:
1-888-383-3110

we bring dreams to life

CPSIA information can be obtained at www.ICGtesting.com
Printed in the USA
BVOW012359210812

298381BV00001B/3/P